STOKOWSKI

Paul Robinson

Discography by Bruce Surtees

Macdonald and Jane's · London

The Art of the Conductor

Also available in this series

KARAJAN

Forthcoming

SOLTI
BERNSTEIN
FURTWÄNGLER

First published in Great Britain in 1977
by Macdonald and Jane's Publishers Limited,
Paulton House, 8 Sheperdess Walk, London N.1.

ISBN 0 354 04232 7

Printed in Great Britain by
Billing and Sons Limited,
London, Guildford and Worcester

Photographs appear after page 76

Preface

This is the second volume in the series *The Art of the Conductor*. If Herbert von Karajan, the subject of the first volume, is the most celebrated of living conductors, Leopold Stokowski ought to be no less famous. His work spans a much longer period and he has made many more recordings. But Stokowski has been in semi-retirement for a number of years. Comparatively few people are familiar with his best recordings — they have been absent from the catalogue for a long time — and fewer still have ever seen him conduct.

While much has been written about Stokowski over the years there is no full-length study of his life and work. This book tries to provide such a study in the conviction that it is long overdue.

In the preparation of this volume I was greatly helped by Paul Hoeffler, some of whose photographs of Stokowski appear in these pages. Paul made available to me a vast number of recordings, tapes, programs, scores and other memorabilia, so that I was able to hear a great many Stokowski performances and interviews covering numerous decades. I am also indebted to Steve Cohen for his comprehensive radio series in Philadelphia which brought to light useful information about Stokowski.

Like the first volume, this book took shape initially as a series of radio broadcasts over CJRT-FM in Toronto. I wish to thank the manager of the station, Cam Finley, and technician Ron Hughes, as well as CJRT's loyal and constructive listeners, who all contributed to the development of the material.

Introduction

What makes a great conductor? Extraordinary musical talent, no doubt, but surely other qualities, shared by all great leaders, are essential as well. Great conductors and great leaders in general have the ability to make others do more than they imagined they ever could in their wildest dreams. Such individuals also commonly possess an unusually powerful vision of what it is they are trying to achieve. Conductors of superiority must have both a singular ability to galvanize their players and a distinguished conception of the scores they perform. A first-class orchestral musician has absolute control of his instrument and knowledge of the entire symphonic repertoire. No conductor tells him how to play his instrument and no conductor really teaches him to play the pieces he has known for years. But it is often the conductor who brings all such knowledge and experience to life as inspired music-making, and only the greatest conductors succeed in doing this with any regularity.

The above, while *describing* in a vague way what conducting is about, does not *explain* it. How, precisely, is inspiration transmitted or elicited? Is it done by means of a technique? If so, is this technique purely musical or of some other kind? Does it, perhaps, resemble an actor's technique which concerns itself with gestures and role-playing, or even a psychologist's, in the sense that a conductor persuades his musicians to respond exactly to his signals? Might there not also be something of the preacher's and the super-salesman's skill in what a great conductor does?

Answers to such questions are beyond the scope of the present book but the possibility that certain great conductors are indebted to some degree to non-musical talents and skills, should be mentioned. Leopold Stokowski is an excellent example. His musical abilities are considerable but do not entirely explain his stature and reputation. In fact, his purely musical talents are even seriously offset by dubious musical judgement. Stokowski is both a musician of uncommon accomplishment and a singular personality. Without putting him "on the couch" it is possible to deduce from the facts of his life that he was always possessed of a desire to dominate. As a musician he never played in an orchestra as one of many, but preferred instead the role of organist, choirmaster and orchestral conductor, and in all three positions he gave the orders. His abrupt departures from important conducting posts throughout his career reinforce the view that he was obsessed with getting his own way. This professional desire to dominate is reflected in his personal life. He was married three times, first to pianist Olga Samaroff, next to Evangeline Johnson (of the Johnson and Johnson empire) and finally to Gloria Vanderbilt. In each case there were children and in each case the women divorced Stokowski. The recurrent complaint was that Stokowski insisted on being the boss. Marriage was an unnatural condition for a man as dedicated to achieving his own goals as Stokowski was. Why he married in the first place and why he repeated the mistake twice more, might have something to do with the fact that the Stokowski brides were extremely well-equipped financially and socially and did no harm to the advancement of his career. Beyond that he seemed to have no need for them at all, and for their part they were unable to find any satisfying role to play in his life.

With the possible exception of his two sons by Gloria Vanderbilt, Stokowski has never appeared to need anyone to relate to on an equal basis. His nature is to draw all he can from others, making them the means to realize his own ends. There is no evidence that Stokowski has ever feared reciprocation, but he has certainly avoided it. Plenty of examples of his great generosity are overshadowed by the persistent image of a powerful personality controlling others. This is entirely appropriate to his profession as a conductor, and the combination of a drive to dominate and a skill capable of achieving domination helps to account for his success.

As a man Stokowski has aspired to the condition of self-sufficiency as a perfectly reasonable and honourable goal for a human being. And yet, how ironic that by definition no conductor can be self-sufficient! A conductor's need for an orchestra is fundamental to his self-realization. Yet Stokowski's view of conducting is far-reaching. It is not irrelevant, for instance, to note his fascination with technical advances in sound and film recording. One suspects that his ideal orchestra would not be human at all but merely an extension of the mixing devices in a recording studio.

The aspiration for self-sufficiency in Stokowski is stressed not to belittle his achievements, but to attempt to understand what kind of man it took to attain them. Stokowski's marriages are mentioned not to descend to gossip at the expense of discussion of his musical activity — to which the main body of the book is almost solely devoted — but to suggest clues to the art of this conductor. The way in which Stokowski controls his life is not dissimilar to the way in which he controls orchestras and scores. Even conducting the most passionate music he seldom surrenders himself to its emotion, thereby creating a sense of distance. Perhaps the obvious eccentricities of many Stokowski performances reflect not so much his feelings about the music but proof of his superiority to, or domination of the composer. These interpretative aberrations, which critics have complained about for decades, are all too often imposed on the music by one who has little respect for its creator, but boundless admiration for his own powers.

As a conductor Stokowski may be remembered for the perversity of many of his interpretations. More likely music-lovers will recall the remarkable Philadelphia Orchestra he built with its unique discipline and tonal palette. But the pervasive and unforgettable quality in all Stokowski performances has been control. He has always prided himself on his mastery not only of himself, his music, his orchestras and his audiences, but of almost everything else important in life. As fascinating evidence of this aspect of Stokowski's personality one need only consult some of the many interviews he has given. No doubt he grew tired of answering the same old questions but his responses are astonishingly similar. Although he is not a man to articulate new ideas spontaneously, one begins to suspect that he had written out and memorized answers to all the standard questions and simply regurgitated them for years afterwards. There is a simplicity about what he has to say that suggests severe limitations of insight. As far back as the 1930s Stokowski was the guru *par excellence* among eminent artists, a man to be consulted on all matters, musical or otherwise. He seemed to enjoy playing this role and adopted a suitably haughty, patrician tone that

6

suggested impatience with fools and others with aspirations to pretensions equalling his own. In spite of his pioneering efforts to reach the masses in youth concerts and in films, Stokowski to this day retains an Olympian aura. He is a stiff, unbending man neither willing nor able to relax, and incapable of being only one of many in any public situation. Again, the obsession with control and domination, both of himself and of others; perhaps a trait which every great conductor must possess — it is certainly characteristic of Stokowski. However, it is not merely the existence of such an obsession that is remarkable — many individuals of modest achievements could be similarly described — but Stokowski's ability to actually attain control and domination. Finally, of course, it is the capacity to wield authority *to some purpose of aesthetic value*, thereby distinguishing him from successful businessmen and politicians, that makes Stokowski the important artist he undoubtedly is.

1
Prelude to Philadelphia

Stokowski has disputed it on several occasions, but it is now established beyond question that he was born April 18, 1882. There appears to be no obvious reason why Stokowski should prefer another date. That he has done so, to the chagrin of several interviewers, reveals something about the man. Like Sir Thomas Beecham, he is prepared to make pronouncements on any subject with complete authority. If the facts seem to point the other way, so much the worse for the facts. Another point of contention over the years has been Stokowski's original name. Some claim that he came into the world with the name Leonard Stokes. Stokowski himself denies this and no one has ever produced sufficient proof to contradict him. In fact, his birth certificate actually reads "Leopold Anthony Stokowski."

Stokowski's father was Polish and his mother Irish. His father's side of the family came to England to escape the Russian Czars, and apparently the dominant culture in the household remained Polish. The elder Stokowski was a cabinet maker by trade and the family lived in Upper Marylebone Street, in the St. John's Wood area of London. Stokowski's earliest musical recollection is hearing a violin for the first time when his grandfather took him to a club. He was seven years old. Stokowski does not seem to have displayed any prodigious musical ability, but he was interested enough to learn to play not only the violin, but viola, cello, piano and organ as well. The organ turned out to be his main instrument and he entered the Royal College of Music in 1895 to study it more intensively. Among his teachers were two of the most prominent English composers of the day: Hubert Parry and Charles Stanford. His student colleagues included such future luminaries as Gustav Holst and Ralph Vaughan Williams.

Although Stokowski's early life was coloured by his father's Polish origins, his most important musical training was a characteristically English one. Those who came into contact with him at that time always took him to be English, although the Stokowski we know certainly does not *sound* English. In fact, his accent defies identification. As long as most people can remember, Stokowski has possessed that peculiar accent with a bizarre propensity to leave out articles in his speech, much like Charlie Chan. Perhaps Stokowski did sound English at one time, but he does no longer. Nor did his musical tastes turn out to be English. Even in his early years as a conductor in America Stokowski did not play much English music and later on it was conspicuous by its absence from his programs.

Stokowski has no sentimentality about the past. When a period in his life is over he goes on to something completely new, almost as if the previous period never existed. He is notoriously impatient with interviewers who ask him about the past. It simply does not interest him. This attitude is reflected in his repertoire. Even in his eighties he was interested in new music, and into his nineties he is recording many works for the first time. Others might have had a sentimental attachment to the music they grew up with but not Stokowski. For him it was only one stage in a career which has known countless stages.

When pressed, Stokowski will relate that one of the most vivid of his early musical recollections is of Hans Richter, who frequently guest conducted in London in the first decade of this century. Stokowski remembers him as "the greatest conductor I ever heard. I learned from him immensely, and I am very grateful to him . . . very sensitive and at the same time enormously powerful." But precisely why did Richter seem so great to Stokowski and what did he learn from the eminent German? Unfortunately, Stokowski cannot or will not say. The most striking of all Stokowski's early memories, however, is his conducting debut at age 12. Stokowski was the pianist in a children's orchestra at the time and the regular conductor was ill. The experience of conducting this orchestra so thrilled the boy, he was unable to sleep after the concert. "From that day I made up my mind to be a conductor."

In 1898 Stokowski joined the Royal College of Organists for a one-year course and attended Queen's College at Oxford University, after which he went to Paris and Berlin for further study, returning to England in 1903 to take up the post of organist at St. Jame's Church in Piccadilly. While this was an important appointment for the 21-year-old Stokowski, he was after something more illustrious. Within two years he became sufficiently respected and well-known to receive an offer from St. Bartholomew's Church in New York. At this point in his career he was torn in two directions. On the one hand the New York job would be a major step forward in his career as an organist. But by this time he was becoming increasingly serious about conducting, taking every opportunity to go to Germany for its study. In the end, Stokowski accepted the offer from New

York, returning to Europe every summer to continue his conducting studies. The attraction in Germany was the legendary conductor of the Berlin Philharmonic and the Leipzig Gewandhaus Orchestra, Artur Nikisch. By all accounts Nikisch was a model of technical wizardry and interpretative integrity. A young conducting student could not have dreamed of a better teacher. It was, perhaps, from Nikisch that Stokowski learned to keep his movements to a minimum. Another one-time student of Nikisch's, Sir Adrian Boult, also emulates his former teacher's conducting reserve, but Boult lacks Stokowski's flair for the dramatic, something the latter may or may not have picked up from Nikisch.

Stokowski arrived in New York in September 1905 to take up his new post as organist and choirmaster at St. Bartholomew's Church. Located at the corner of Madison and 44th and, at that time, one of the wealthiest in the city, the church was torn down in 1918. Stokowski made the most of what he had to work with, mounting performances of Bach's *St. Matthew Passion* and trying out some compositions of his own on the choir. A piece called *Benedicte* was published. Former members of the choir at St. Bartholomew's recall Stokowski as being a hard taskmaster and rather too arrogant for his age. He would sit motionless at the organ after a postlude, as if in a trance. It is the fate of church organists that they be heard and not seen, for in the context of a church service it seems somehow inappropriate to give a performance in the concert hall sense. Stokowski was simply not the self-effacing church organist type and he was obviously headed for trouble. He resigned from St. Bartholomew's in 1908 and went back to Europe determined to make his way as a conductor.

For the next few years Stokowski continued his studies as a conductor doing his best with what conducting opportunities he could find. For a time he lived in

Paris and made some money by accompanying singers at the piano. With whatever money he had he hired an orchestra so he could conduct, hoping that somebody of importance might see him and offer him a job. That is exactly what happened at a 1909 concert in Paris. In the audience, for the express purpose of scouting Stokowski as a conductor for their newly reorganized orchestra, were two representatives of the Cincinnati Symphony. These men were very impressed with the enterprising, blond, young man, and engaged him as conductor of the Cincinnati for the fall.

The gods must have been smiling on Stokowski that day. There is no doubt that he had talent, but he had had very little experience, and none of the preparation usually associated with a conducting career, never having either played in an orchestra or worked as a coach in an opera house. Apparently, Stokowski had decided that if he had it in him to be a conductor, he need not bother working his way through the usual apprenticeship. So, with phenomenal innocence and arrogance, he presented himself to the Parisian public as Leopold Stokowski, conductor. And the result was not an assistant conductorship with a small orchestra or opera house, but the directorship of an orchestra in a big American city. Not bad for a young man of 27.

Cincinnati provided Stokowski with an extraordinary opportunity. With virtually no experience behind him, he had his own orchestra. It was not the equal of the Berlin Philharmonic or the Boston Symphony, but it was fully professional and it was his. The orchestra, founded in 1895, was inoperative from 1907 to 1909 due to lack of funds. Another attempt was being made to get it going again in the 1909-10 season with 20 concerts. Stokowski has always relished the job of building an orchestra from scratch and he has done it many times since. A born leader, he is the sort of man who likes to have a hand in everything and to make things happen. He sees what needs doing and he marshals the energies and the money to get the job done. In Cincinnati, Stokowski steadily increased the number of concerts from 20 his first year to 26 his second year and 30 his last year. He rehearsed and lectured tirelessly and attracted to Cincinnati leading soloists such as Fritz Kreisler, Mischa Elman, Wilhelm Backhaus and Sergei Rachmaninoff. Somehow he also found time to design the stage and the acoustical shell for Emory Auditorium, the orchestra's home from 1911. With the orchestra he was a dictator, threatening dismissal if the playing was not up to his standard. With the audience he was equally severe. When a 1911 Cincinnati audience rustled its programs too loudly to suit him he reprimanded them sharply:

> Please don't do that! We must have the proper atmosphere.... I do not want to scold you or appear disagreeable.... We work hard all week to give you this music, but I cannot do my best without your aid. I'll give you my best or I won't give you anything. It is for you to choose. (David Ewen, *Dictators of the Baton*. Chicago: Ziff-Davis, 1945, p. 73)

Cincinnati seemed to be the logical place for Stokowski to settle down and grow with the orchestra. After all, he needed time to learn the vast repertoire an orchestral conductor must command. He also needed to acquire experience with an orchestra, something every budding conductor, no matter how great his inborn musical ability, requires in order to refine his stick technique and to develop his understanding of the instruments of the orchestra, individually and collectively. But in 1912, at the end of his third season in Cincinnati, Stokowski suddenly resigned. He complained that he could no longer progress because the board insisted on making all the decisions, never in fact made any, and so as a result nothing got done.

Stokowski's resignation caused turmoil in musical circles in Cincinnati. He had made himself indispensable. The public was on his side and urged him to reconsider; the members of the orchestra pleaded with him; even the board promised to give him whatever he wanted. However, Stokowski turned a deaf ear to everyone claiming that his enthusiasm for the job had been destroyed and could never be restored.

Stokowski was a man in a hurry as evidenced by his career record to that point. Nonetheless, many found his reasons for leaving Cincinnati puzzling and unconvincing. When Stokowski's appointment to head the Philadelphia Orchestra was announced a few months later, it appeared that he had been playing games. Did he have the Philadelphia contract in his pocket when he precipitated a feud with his board in Cincinnati? The circumstances strongly suggest it but Stokowski himself has always denied it.

2
The Philadelphia Story

In 1912 when Stokowski took over the Philadelphia Orchestra, it was far from being one of the better orchestras in America, let alone one of the best in the world. It is one of his greatest achievements that when he left it 25 years later, the Philadelphia Orchestra had no equal anywhere.

The Philadelphia Orchestra was formed in 1900, long after the New York Philharmonic, the Chicago Symphony and the Boston Symphony. Its first conductor was German-born Fritz Scheel, already resident in the city as leader of a number of amateur groups. Born in Lübeck in 1852, Scheel had held a variety of minor appointments all over Germany, had worked for some years with Hans von Bülow in Hamburg, and could boast of meeting Brahms, Tchaikovsky and Anton Rubinstein. Scheel was an excellent musician and just the man to create a professional orchestra where none had existed before. In the beginning, Scheel naturally recruited players from Europe where the traditions of orchestral playing were stronger and where Scheel himself had good connections. The players invited to Philadelphia during these years were mostly German

15

but the concertmaster was Scottish.

The orchestra began with a series of 14 subscription concert pairs, giving a total of 52 concerts in all the first season. The young orchestra also felt ready to undertake some modest touring, visiting Boston, New York and smaller cities within a reasonable distance. Richard Strauss came to conduct his own music and so did Rachmaninoff and Felix Weingartner.

But by 1906 it was evident that Scheel was not in the best of health. His behaviour became so irrational, he had to be confined to an institution where he died in 1907. There were many tributes paid him but none more significant than a comment from Stokowski some years later:

> The man who really made the Philadelphia Orchestra from a musical standpoint was Fritz Scheel. I never knew him personally but he must have had very high musical ideals. Such artists as Rich, Horner and Schwar, to mention only a few of the many who are still remaining in the Philadelphia Orchestra from Fritz Scheel's time, are absolutely in the first rank for their instrument, not only in America but in the whole world.

Unfortunately, Scheel's development of the orchestra was not continued by his successor. Carl Pohlig came from a background very similar to Scheel's, but was apparently not in the same class either as a person or as a musician, managing somehow to antagonize everyone — the players, the audiences and the critics. When Pohlig appeared in New York with the orchestra in 1907 the reviews were brutal. In June 1912, Pohlig's resignation was announced and he was paid off with a full year's salary of $12,000.

Pohlig's deficiencies were well-known to the board of the Philadelphia Orchestra early in his tenure, but they had difficulty replacing him. Pohlig was retained only until a better conductor could be found. This is where Stokowski came in. Fresh from his break with the Cin-

16

cinnati Symphony in the spring of 1912, Stokowski was available, and he looked attractive enough to cause Pohlig to be removed a year ahead of schedule.

History has proven that the board of the Philadelphia Orchestra made the wisest choice possible in hiring Stokowski. But why was this man so special, even then? Why had the Cincinnati Symphony hired him when he was almost totally lacking in experience? It seems that whatever Stokowski lacked in experience he more than made up for in personal magnetism. When he stood in front of an orchestra attention naturally flowed to him both from the orchestra and the audience. This is borne out by a review of a concert Stokowski gave in London in 1912 within a few months of his appointment to the Philadelphia Orchestra:

> This program was evidently designed chiefly with the object of showing his powers in various directions, for it contained familiar works which are, as it were, a conductor's test pieces. A conductor must prove his power in three directions: he must show that he knows what he wants, that he can secure it from the players, and most important of all, he has to convince his hearers of the fitness of his judgement.... Mr. Stokowski gave absolute assurance at once. The fact that he conducted the Overture [Wagner, *Die Meistersinger*] and the Symphony [Brahms, Symphony No. 1] from memory would not in itself count for very much but his thorough knowledge of the music and of his own intention with regard to it was shown in the instant response to his requirements. (*Times of London*)

This concert also featured the great violin virtuoso Efrem Zimbalist playing the Glazunov Concerto, and in the audience that night was another distinguished violinist, Joseph Szigeti:

> I still remember the already then typically Stokowskian sound of the London Symphony Orchestra in the concluding number — Tchaikovsky's *Marche Slave* — and the feline suppleness of the orchestral support that the young conductor gave to Zimbalist's playing of Glazunov's Concerto, then still a comparative novelty. (Joseph Szigeti, *With Strings Attached*. New York: Knopf, 1947, p. 244)

17

In 1912 the Philadelphia Orchestra was still very much the creation of its first conductor Fritz Scheel. Its members were largely German, its two conductors had been German, and in fact German was the language spoken at rehearsals even in Stokowski's early years with the orchestra. It was expected that another German *Kapellmeister* would be hired to replace the disappointing Carl Pohlig, yet to almost everyone's surprise, Stokowski got the job. It is true that he had studied with Nikisch, the leading German conductor of the day, but Stokowski's training was mostly in England and his experience largely in the United States. Again, one can only conclude that Stokowski's talent and charisma were so great, the "old boy" network which had prevailed in Philadelphia was set aside.

In October 1912 Stokowski made his debut in Philadelphia with a program cannily designed to emphasize brilliance and excitement: Wagner's *Tannhäuser* Overture, Beethoven's *Leonore* No. 3 Overture, Ippolitov-Ivanov's *Caucasian Sketches*, and Brahms Symphony No. 1. Each of these works is scored for a large orchestra and each ends in a climax louder and more thrilling than the preceding one. With the exception of the Ippolitov-Ivanov, which was receiving its first performance in the United States, this was a program any German conductor might have presented in 1912. It would be misleading, therefore, to suggest that Stokowski initially represented a new direction for the orchestra. However, after several years of mediocrity under Pohlig, Stokowski's debut was eagerly anticipated. He did not disappoint the orchestra; nor did he displease the music critic of the *Public Ledger*:

> Stokowski came forward with bowed head, evidently pondering the content of his musical message. Those who went forth to see a hirsute eccentricity were disappointed. They beheld a surprisingly boyish and thoroughly businesslike figure who was sure of

himself, yet free from conceit, who dispensed with the score by virtue of an infallible memory, and held his men and his audience from the first note to the last firmly in his grasp.... Mr. Stokowski's conducting is after the order of Nikisch, whom he frankly admires.... His gestures are graphic, the arcs and parabolas he describes tell of a kind of geometrical translation going on in his mind, whereby he visualizes the confluent rhythms in outward action. (*Philadelphia Public Ledger*, Oct. 12, 1912)

Another review of the same concert in the *Evening Bulletin* saw in Stokowski "no excess of temperament," and detected a deportment denoting "refinement, seriousness, studious love of his work, and sane, sensible ideas." These reviews seem somewhat ironic today. Stokowski's interpretations over the years have been perceived by many people as just the opposite of "sane" or "sensible." Yet most of Stokowski's early reviews in London, New York and Philadelphia are in agreement on this point. It could be that styles of performance have changed, and that what appears wilful today might have seemed perfectly straightforward in 1912. Or, it could be argued that Stokowski gradually became more free in his interpretations over the years. Support for this view comes from Saul Caston, solo trumpet in the Philadelphia for many years and later a conductor himself.

I admired the old Stokowski when his interpretations were 1% Stokowski and 99% the composer. Later it became 99% Stokowski and 1% the composer.

Perhaps the truth lies somewhere in between. Since Stokowski did not begin recording until 1917, it is difficult to be sure. On the evidence of the recordings from the acoustical era (1917-1925) Stokowski's emergence as a conductor with a fondness for tampering with a score was relatively slow. The most bizarre interpretations occur after the Philadelphia years

19

(1912-1940) when he may have been growing tired of doing the same old thing.

Stokowski's first impression on Philadelphia was a very positive one, demonstrating from the beginning that he was a master conductor in absolute control of himself, the orchestra and the repertoire. Within a short time Philadelphians were also made aware of his ambition and his curiosity about new music. During his first five years in Philadelphia he conducted the American premières of numerous major works including Richard Strauss' *Alpine* Symphony, Mahler's Symphony No. 8, Mahler's *Das Lied von der Erde* and Scriabin's *Poem of Ecstasy*. The audiences, however, were not entirely pleased with this heavy dose of new music. Nor were the critics. In 1915 Stokowski gave the first American performance of Schoenberg's *Chamber* Symphony No. 1, in Philadelphia, and then later in New York. Held in the ballroom of the Ritz-Carlton Hotel, the concert was performed under the auspices of the Society of the Friends of New Music. Here is one critic's reaction:

> Music that has been veiled to one generation has often been revealed to the next as a clear and intelligible advance. But it does not necessarily follow that every toad, ugly and venomous, wears yet a precious jewel in his head and that all repellent music contains hidden beauties waiting to be revealed. The *Kammersymphonie* did not yesterday show the prescience of a master, the vision of a seer into unknown realms of beauty. Will our grandchildren see it and smile indulgently at the bewildered listeners of 1915? The question is not really important: bewildered listeners of 1915 can only listen for themselves. Mr. Stokowski conducted an admirable performance of this difficult and complicated work with apparent enthusiasm and belief. (Richard Aldrich, *Concert Life in New York 1902-1923*. New York: Putnam's, 1941, p. 477)

The players in the Philadelphia Orchestra soon found that their new conductor was interested not only in new repertoire, but also in improving the quality of the orchestra. For many of them this meant trouble. In one season Stokowski fired no fewer than 36 players. For those who remained, work under Stokowski was more demanding than it had ever been before. He knew what he wanted and was not satisfied until he got it. Often each member of the violin or cello sections would be made to play his part alone, and then endure Stokowski's criticism of the performance in front of the entire orchestra. His attitude also annoyed many players. Maintaining a certain distance from his men at all times, Stokowski never addressed them by their first names if he addressed them by name at all, and they certainly did not address him as anything other than "Mr. Stokowski." He discouraged small talk and players who wished to have a conversation with him were required to make an appointment with his secretary. At rehearsals Stokowski was demanding but not in the Toscanini manner of losing his temper or even raising his voice. Stokowski got what he wanted by maintaining his own self-control and by persistence. He was notorious for keeping after a player or a problem until it was solved, whereas other conductors might have let it go after a few repetitions.

It may seem contradictory that Stokowski would pay tribute to his predecessor Fritz Scheel for bringing to the orchestra a great number of its best players, and then set about to fire so many of them. But Stokowski preserved only what was first-class in the orchestra and ruthlessly got rid of the rest as soon as possible. In terms of building an orchestra he knew exactly what he was doing and within a few years, had raised the quality of the orchestra beyond recognition. Among the players he retained from the Scheel years was Anton Horner. This remarkable musician, who joined the orchestra in 1902 and retired in 1946, was the first horn player for 28 years. Considering the four horn players remained unchanged for a period of more than 20 years under

21

Stokowski, he must have had a special sympathy for them. Another Scheel import who lasted a long time during Stokowski's tenure was the timpanist Oscar Schwar.

Many of the players Stokowski brought into the orchestra in his first years were imported from France. Foremost among them was the principal oboist Marcel Tabuteau who stayed for many years in the Philadelphia, establishing the style and standard of playing for several generations of oboists. During the heyday of the Philadelphia Orchestra under Stokowski, leading players in the orchestra became as famous in musical circles as star baseball players in the sports field. In addition to Horner, Schwar and Tabuteau, there was solo cellist Hans Kindler, principal double bassist Antonio Torello from Spain, concertmaster Alexander Hilsberg from Manchuria, and two Americans, flautist William Kincaid and trumpeter Saul Caston. The careers of these last two typically reflect Stokowski's method of building the orchestra. Kincaid came into the orchestra in 1920 and stayed for 40 years as principal flute; Caston arrived in 1918 at the age of 17 and was still there well into the Ormandy era. The length of tenure of so many of these players is profound evidence of Stokowski's ability to choose exactly the player he wanted from an audition. He has the uncanny power to be able to determine not only technical facility, but also how well a sound will blend with the rest of the orchestra, and whether a player's musicianship is compatible with his own. It is also apparent that the astonishing homogeneity of sound and flexibility of phrasing which the Philadelphia Orchestra possessed in the 1930s was just as much the result of their having played together for many years as of Stokowski's conducting.

This brings up the matter of the "Philadelphia Sound." Most people agree that the sound of the

Philadelphia under Stokowski was unique. There was an opulence, especially in the strings, that persists to this day, even though Eugene Ormandy has been its conductor for more than 30 years. The orchestra's sound, rich in the manner of an organ, with slow-moving chords perfectly balanced and sustained effortlessly over a powerful bass, reflected Stokowski's taste in music, of which his transcriptions of organ works by Bach provide excellent examples. These transcriptions take advantage of the infinite range of colour and dynamics of the modern orchestra, while preserving something of the sustaining power, clarity of line and grandeur of the organ. It has been said that Stokowski is more interested in sound than in music, the scores of Bach, Beethoven and Brahms simply being vehicles for his sound-sculpting. There is no question that Stokowski is obsessed with the sheer sound of an orchestra, certainly more so than other conductors of his era such as Felix Weingartner or Pierre Monteux. But Stokowski is also an interpreter of distinction, at least in music that interests him. Besides, beauty of sound and meticulous control of timbre in an orchestra are often the key to a successful performance. The "Philadelphia Sound" may be too much of a good thing in Handel, Mozart or even Beethoven, but in the romantic and impressionist composers (Richard Strauss, Rachmaninoff, Debussy and Ravel), it can be ideal.

How did Stokowski achieve the "Philadelphia Sound?" One of the secrets was the concept of free bowing. Most orchestral parts contain bowing instructions which indicate when the strings are to change from up bow to down bow and so forth, so that all players in a section will be moving the bow in the same direction at the same time. This is of enormous help in matters of precision. But Stokowski believed that this very precision often got in the way of the music. Just when a phrase required more volume or more richness of tone, players had to change the direction of the bow and so failed to produce the required sound. His solution was to ask players to change bows at different times, thus eliminating breaks in the line and allowing for a more constant and seamless flow of tone. This technique was used for years in Philadelphia and is responsible for some of the orchestra's most beautiful effects. Although the results of Stokowski's use of free bowing have been widely admired, the technique is not practised extensively today, not even in the Philadelphia Orchestra. Free bowing is apt to cause confusion in an orchestra, and many players and conductors doubt that it is really needed, when the same effects can invariably be achieved using the old-fashioned strict bowing.

While the technique of free-bowing is renowned as a Stokowski innovation in Philadelphia, it is far less well-known that he tried to achieve similar effects with wind and brass players. Stokowski soon learned to his dismay that wind players had the unfortunate habit of taking a breath and thereby breaking the line of a phrase. Most conductors took this to be a fact of life, but not Stokowski who wanted the same seamless tone in the winds and brass that he could achieve in the strings with free bowing. To do this he added extra musicians to the orchestra for the purpose of bridging the gaps. Unlike the large string section in which many players could continue a phrase while others changed bow, in the winds and brass there was customarily only one player to a part. If he paused to take a breath, there was simply no music. Stokowski's solution was to double up wherever possible so that during a breath another player could take over. By this means, the orchestra could achieve long, seamless *crescendos* and avoid false accents in the middle of a phrase.

Another secret of the "Philadelphia Sound" was

24

Stokowski's approach to a score and the way in which he communicated his thoughts to the orchestra through words and gesture. He always came to rehearsals with a concept in sound of what he wanted, and often insisted on achieving it no matter what the technical problem for an instrumentalist. It frequently happened that a player would find what Stokowski wanted impossible. Stokowski's advice, that the player "go home and think about it and come back tomorrow," usually solved the problem. More often than not, the musician in question worked like a demon and came back able to do exactly what Stokowski had demanded. Stokowski has an enormous knowledge of the technical capabilities of the instruments of the orchestra but prefers to use non-technical language in rehearsal, often speaking in images and philosophical ideas to generate the desired response. However, he achieves at least as much with gesture. Unlike most conductors, past and present, Stokowski preferred to conduct without a baton after 1926, and it is easy to see why. He has an extraordinary gift for evoking sounds through gesture. Critics have accused him of designing his movements to please the audience, but the players in the Philadelphia Orchestra felt otherwise. They realized that it was a great innovation for a conductor to try to communicate so much with his hands, and once they got used to it they found it remarkably helpful. Stokowski likes to improvise during a concert, making changes in tempo or balance as the mood takes him, and he can do this successfully only because his gestures are so clear and precise. For example, he will indicate softer or louder to the second horn or third clarinet just by raising or lowering the appropriate finger.

Stokowski's experiments with the seating arrangement of the orchestra also contributed to the "Philadelphia Sound." The standard orchestral seating plan still widely used today is to have strings spread out to either side of the conductor at the edge of the stage, with winds, brass and percussion behind them, usually on a series of platforms. This arrangement is thought to produce the best possible balance. But Stokowski was not satisfied with it, and tried many set-ups, his most famous alternative being to bring the winds to the front of the stage, moving the strings behind for a change.

The traditional seating came down to us from the small orchestra of Haydn's time: the large, modern symphonic orchestra must adapt itself to quite different acoustical problems. (Stokowski in a letter to the editor of *High Fidelity/Musical America*, July 1969)

Unfortunately, as Stokowski knows all too well, there are as many ideas about the proper sound of a symphony orchestra as there are conductors and musicians. Some prefer a homogeneous blend in which nothing is too prominent, while others are partial to a sound in which each instrument is clearly distinguishable. Then there is the problem of what is appropriate to each composer; the balance suitable to Mozart is not right for Wagner. Finally, the size and character of the concert hall itself must be taken into account. No one has been more sensitive to problems of balance and acoustics than Stokowski. It is, perhaps, the lesson of his lifetime of experimentation that other conductors should try to be more sensitive to these problems and more flexible as they move from one composer or from one hall to another.

Stokowski's innovations in Philadelphia were not limited to sound experimentation. He began Pops concerts in 1915 and Young People's Concerts in 1921. In this latter field his most refreshing change was the introduction in 1930 of Youth Concerts aimed at young people between the ages of 13 and 25. The idea for these concerts grew out of an awareness of the particularly discouraging effect the Depression was having on young people. Stokowski was a great man to the youth of Philadelphia and he realized that perhaps he could lead them where others had failed. He believed that what they needed was to get involved in something worthwhile which they had helped create themselves. With this as a guiding principle, the organization for the Youth Concerts was carried on by student volunteers. Tickets for these Saturday afternoon concerts were inexpensive, ranging from 10 cents to 75 cents in 1932, and most interesting of all, no adult was admitted unless accompanied by 10 children. For the establishment-oriented Philadelphia Orchestra to take such an interest in the welfare of disadvantaged youth was unprecedented. Stokowski was rewarded by developing an enormous and devoted following, certain members of which were not beyond going to his house and serenading him after a concert. For his part, he said that he regarded the young people as guinea-pigs, trying out new ideas and new repertoire on them with his orchestra before attempting to interest their parents. Stokowski had a lot in common with youth. Like them, he had few pre-conceptions about what music had value or what was possible in a concert hall. They were his natural constituency, comprising a far more responsive audience than the archly conservative Friday afternoon crowd. The Youth Concerts were presented about every six weeks during the season, and orchestra and conductor donated their services. It must be stressed that these were not concerts devoted to the lesser or more obvious pieces in the repertoire. Full-scale affairs peppered with modern works, they featured big-name soloists like Kirsten Flagstad and Jascha Heifetz as well as gifted youth soloists such as the 15-year old Eugene List who made his debut in the American première of the Shostakovich Piano Concerto No. 1.

Stokowski was so taken with the enthusiasm and talent of young people, he spent many hours promoting the idea of a Youth Centre with its own orchestra, chorus, theatre and more. Nor was his interest in youth a passing fancy. During the Second World War he organized and conducted the All-American Youth Orchestra; still later he founded the youthful American Symphony.

Most of the Stokowski "events" in Philadelphia were related to the performance of particular pieces, usually premières. In 1916, for example, he chose to perform Mahler's Symphony No. 8, the so-called *Symphony of a Thousand*, because of the number of performers required. Stokowski had heard Mahler himself rehearse the work in Munich and could not wait to introduce it to American audiences. At that time, Mahler was anything but a popular composer and the board of the Philadelphia Orchestra was not about to lay out $14,000 to play his music. But Stokowski was an uncompromising and persuasive man and in April 1916 the Philadelphia Orchestra gave nine sold-out performances of the work in Philadelphia and another in New York at the Metropolitan Opera House. As Stokowski had predicted there was even a small profit on the venture. The critics were somewhat perplexed by the structure and the meaning of the huge symphony, but full of praise for Stokowski:

> It is not easy to see in this composition the really potent achievement of a creative imagination. It seems rather the high aspiration of a musician ... whose lofty ambitions are not matched by his inspiration....The performance ...was little short of magnificent....The orchestral portion of the work was played with entire mastery....Mr Stokowski gave evidence of his high abilities as a conductor by his preparation of such a performance and his firm command of all the forces under his baton. He conducted the work without a score. (Aldrich, *Concert Life in New York, 1902-1923,* p. 509)

28

In addition to the Mahler Eighth and the works mentioned earlier as being premièred during Stokowski's first five years in Philadelphia, there were a host of others introduced to America or the world by Stokowski. Sergei Koussevitzky in Boston might have played more new works by American composers, but Stokowski played more new works, period. He knew personally the leading composers of the day and made a point of learning their music and giving it the best possible performance. He met Shostakovich in Russia in the 1920s at a time when the young composer was all but unknown. Stokowski gave the first American performance of Shostakovich's First Symphony and also made the first recording of the work with the Philadelphia Orchestra. After meeting Sibelius in Finland, he returned to give the first American performances of the Symphonies No. 5, 6 and 7, and to make the first recording of the Symphony No. 4 in 1932. He knew Prokofiev in Paris in his student days ("very simple, childlike but with caustic humour") and premièred his ballet *The Age of Steel* in 1931. The list goes on and on to include Schoenberg's *Gurrelieder*, Elgar's *Enigma* Variations, Rachmaninoff's Symphony No. 3, Stravinsky's *Le Sacre du Printemps* and Berg's opera *Wozzeck* — all of them given for the first time in the United States by Leopold Stokowski.

The most spectacular series of Stokowski premières were given under the auspices of the League of Composers and might have begun as early as 1925 but for a rivalry with the International Composer's Guild. This latter was a group run by composer Edgar Varèse, and Stokowski had formed a relationship with both the composer and his organization. The League of Composers decided to mount a production of Manuel de Falla's puppet opera *El Retaldo* and approached Stokowski to conduct. He responded by asking the

League to relinquish rights to the first performance to the Guild with whom Stokowski had previously promised to do the work. The League stood its ground, having obtained the rights fairly and squarely through the good offices of harpsichordist Wanda Landowska. The man who ended up conducting the première was not Stokowski, but an equally illustrious colleague named Willem Mengelberg, then the conductor of the New York Philharmonic. Stokowski and the League finally got together for the first time with a production of Stravinsky's *Les Noces* in 1928 given in the Metropolitan Opera House in New York. This was the beginning of many such productions involving Stokowski and the League. It was also to be the first of only two rather brief periods in Stokowski's life when he got involved with opera. Stokowski, notorious for wanting to control everything he was involved in, often antagonized either people intent on the same thing, or others satisfied simply with their own area of expertise. For the production of *Les Noces* Serge Soudeikine was in charge of sets, costumes and lighting and he and Stokowski were in nearly constant disagreement. Soudeikine wanted to light his sets and costumes to best advantage, while it was Stokowski's desire to co-ordinate the lighting with the development of the music. However, the real problem turned out to be neither Soudeikine's intransigence nor Stokowski's meddling, but the inadequacies of the Metropolitan's electrical equipment. An unusual feature of *Les Noces* is that it is scored for four pianos. For this production Stokowski had at his keyboards four leading American composers: Aaron Copland, Marc Blitzstein, Louis Gruenberg and Frederick Jacobi.

Notwithstanding the difficulties Stokowski precipitated for the League, he was back again the following year for a production of Stravinsky's ballet score *Le Sacre du Printemps*. There were three performances in

Philadelphia and two in New York, all with Stokowski and the Philadelphia Orchestra. Although the manager of the Orchestra, Arthur Judson, tried to discourage the project, especially when he heard that Schoenberg's *Die Glückliche Hand* was also to be on the program, Stokowski prevailed as he so often did when he committed himself to a project. When the rehearsals began there were the inevitable conflicts between Stokowski and other members of the production staff. This time the major disputes were with Leonide Massine, who had choreographed the original Diaghilev production in Paris, and the solo dancer Martha Graham. The three of them argued endlessly about interpretation and tempo, with Stokowski and Graham invariably taking one side against Massine. There was even a last-minute uproar about the proper length of the women's skirts in the ballet!

For all the difficulties, however, the production was a great success. Stokowski did not get into arguments with everyone involved; on the contrary he got on famously with the stage director Robert Jones, of whom he said: "We worked like two brothers. With so little he expressed so much." The two of them went on to collaborate on other productions, including Stravinsky's *Oedipus Rex*, Prokofiev's *Age of Steel*, and Schoenberg's *Pierrot Lunaire*. This last was given in Town Hall, New York in 1932 at a time when the League was forced to limit itself to small-scale productions in the light of unfavourable financial conditions. Making a virtue of necessity, Jones and Stokowski produced one of their most imaginative ventures. The small ensemble with Stokowski conducting was placed on the far left of the stage, practically in darkness except for lights on the music stands. In order to achieve even greater darkness, Stokowski had the music photostated on black paper with the notes in white, reducing the lighting on the stands even more. At center stage sat the Pierrot, Mina Hager, in much brighter light. The effect was enhanced still further by covering the musician's white collars with black cloth.

Stokowski became so fascinated with opera and musical theatre during the years he was involved in these League of Composers productions, he seriously considered starting an opera company of his own. But the beginning of the Depression was not the time to do it. Stokowski did not turn again to opera for more than a quarter of a century when he conducted at the New York City Opera and at the Met. Unquestionably, however, Stokowski's major operatic triumph in his earlier period was not with the League of Composers but with the Philadelphia Orchestra in the 1931 American première of Berg's *Wozzeck* at the Academy of Music, with a cast which included Nelson Eddy as the Drum Major. Unfortunately, the production is most remembered for the lighting which threw grotesque shadows of the conductor's moving hands on the walls and ceiling. While this aspect of the production may have been accidental, Stokowski's enemies took it to typify his need to be the centre of attention; a somewhat unfair criticism considering how hard Stokowski worked to present new and difficult music. A *prima donna* he certainly was, but it is to his credit that he used his star quality and popular appeal to further the cause of contemporary music.

While Stokowski's interest in new music made him a rarity among conductors, he was also unique in his great attraction to new technology in terms of what it could do for music. He believed in the value of recordings at a time when they were pretty awful.

> At first I refused to make records because they were so terrible. I refused to distort the music. But then I realized how foolish I had been. I decided I should make the records and try to find out why they were bad.

Just when he began to lose heart that they would ever get better near the end of the acoustical era, the electrical microphone was invented, and a whole new world of sound reproduction opened. The creation of the long-playing record, the tape recorder and stereophonic sound were to help raise the quality of recorded sound even higher, and Stokowski was around for each of these breakthroughs, always among the first to take advantage of the new techniques. At one point in the Philadelphia years he asked Bell Laboratories to try to improve his recordings. Bell installed a studio under the stage of the Academy of Music to experiment as much as it liked with recording. Stokowski also worked tirelessly to solve problems of transmitting concerts by radio.

Stokowski's interest was not limited to the standard symphony orchestra. In the 1920s he organized a band which, of course, turned out to be the best band anyone could remember hearing. One perceptive observer, H.L. Mencken, offered this comment:

> Stokowski has neither tried to batter his audience into unconsciousness with mere noise, in the manner of the Italian conductors, nor endeavored to make his band an imitation orchestra, in the fashion of John Philip Sousa. Instead he has sought, within the natural limits of his medium, to augment its flexibility, its variety, its dignity — in brief, to convert it into a first-rate musical instrument. I can only report that the results he achieves are *kolossal*. Here, at last, is a brass band that can play Bach! (H.L. Mencken, *On Music*. New York: Knopf, 1961, p. 122)

While Stokowski was conductor of the Philadelphia Orchestra, there were the inevitable rumours from time to time that he was leaving to take over another orchestra, the most persistent of which had him succeeding Walter Damrosch as conductor of the New York Symphony in 1928. This never happened but speculation continued, especially when Stokowski had a spectacular success in New York, which was nearly every time he conducted a concert there. On one of the most memorable of such occasions, Stokowski conducted Wagner's *Magic Fire Music* with a huge orchestra which included 50 men each from the New York Symphony, the New York Philharmonic and the Philadelphia Orchestra — 150 players in all! In 1930 there was an extraordinary series of concerts in both New York and Philadelphia in which Stokowski and Toscanini exchanged podiums, Stokowski conducting Toscanini's New York Philharmonic and Toscanini conducting the Philadelphia Orchestra. Prior to the exchange, a vigorous rivalry had developed between the two orchestras, and music-lovers tended to extol the virtues of the one at the expense of the other, with the critics and even the members of the two orchestras getting involved. As things turned out, Toscanini got much the better of the deal. *New York Times* critic Olin Downes generously found Stokowski "completely different from Toscanini but equal," while to the members of the New York Philharmonic Stokowski was not only different but terrible. They complained that he was hard to follow because he did not use a baton, and because he had no beat. Others resented the way he issued short, crisp demands, while still others found him cold and impersonal. According to timpanist Saul Goodman who was in the Philharmonic at the time and agreed with the critics, many players left the stage and refused to play under Stokowski.

Although he had his ups and downs in New York, Stokowski was the toast of Philadelphia. Most of the players in the Philadelphia Orchestra thought the world of him and audiences looked up to him both as a great conductor and a pillar of the community. And so he was. By temperament and by choice Stokowski was a sophisticated man, completely at home in the company of the rich and the powerful. He created and maintained a social gulf between himself and his players, aligning himself with the members of the board and their circle of friends. Dressing like a banker and discussing financial matters with ease, Stokowski could be as fastidious and as organized as any of them. To Stokowski's great advantage, the board considered him not only a fine musician, but also a man who understood the social milieu in which the orchestra functioned, something which made it all the more difficult for them to say no when he came to them with one of his more outrageous requests.

Stokowski and the board of the Philadelphia Orchestra enjoyed a long and nearly ideal relationship. For more than 20 years Stokowski worked to make the Philadelphia Orchestra the best in the world and to turn the city into a place where the most important musical events took place. For its part, the members of the board did everything they could to find the money to make these achievements possible. Then came the Depression. The board, caught in a squeeze between Stokowski and his endless dreams and the difficulty of finding money in such troubled times, acted in desperation just prior to the 1933 season. Without consulting Stokowski, they voted for a new musical policy, announcing that "music for the coming season will be drawn almost entirely from the traditional repertoire. In times such as these people prefer music which they know and love. Performances of debatable music should be postponed to a more suitable time." Some members of the board, having felt for a long time that Stokowski played too much new music and made too many demands on them, found in the depressed state of the economy, the excuse they needed to bring Stokowski to heel. On the other hand, it was certainly true that audiences were less able just then to afford tickets to a concert, which meant a decline in revenue for the orchestra. It made sense to try to make the concerts more attractive by programming music of greater public appeal. But Stokowski was furious about what the board had done and made an announcement of his own. He told the press:

> For the coming season I have programmed both old and new music. New works will appear at the end of the program so that those who don't like it can leave.

At the very first concert of the season Stokowski played a new work by Werner Josten called *Jungle*. In fact, he played it twice in case the audience had trouble understanding it the first time. Many chose to leave before even one performance and there was a near-stampede prior to the second. But Stokowski was a stubborn man and was not about to knuckle under to any demands from the board that he avoid contemporary music. The financial crisis worsened, however, and Stokowski found himself thwarted at every turn: his plans to tour Russia in 1933-34 with the orchestra were turned down; a whole series of tours to South America, Europe and the Far East over the next four years were rejected; and invitations to conductors such as Bruno Walter and Wilhelm Furtwängler to appear as guests with the orchestra were deemed too expensive. It was all too much for Stokowski after having everything his own way for so long, and he resigned December 6, 1934. This action provoked a full-scale crisis which had the result of bringing terrific public pressure on the board to meet Stokowski's demands. A "Subscribers Emergency Committee" was formed to provide a focus for public outrage and within a few weeks, four of Stokowski's most outspoken opponents on the board were forced to resign. On December 15 the board officially invited Stokowski to return on his own terms.

Stokowski agreed to stay on and the crisis was over — or at least so it seemed.

In 1936 Stokowski again resigned and this time there was no public outcry. It was apparent now that he was not just trying to get his own way; he wanted out altogether. Members of the orchestra recall that Stokowski was bored and restless and he himself said much the same thing. He wanted to travel and "study other musical languages," to make some acoustical experiments, and to investigate the potential of the movies. Stokowski did all of these things over the next few years, including a great deal of travel to the Middle East, Bali and Japan. But he also maintained an involvement with the Philadelphia Orchestra, sharing conducting with Eugene Ormandy, then becoming simply a guest conductor. Even after Ormandy took over, the board tried to get Stokowski to remain closely bound to the orchestra but he refused. It was inexplicable to many that a great conductor in his prime could walk away from the incomparable orchestra he had created, especially when he did not have another orchestra to go to.

Stokowski's critics have always been unwilling to take Stokowski's explanations at face value, and his departure from Philadelphia gave rise to all sorts of speculation. One story had it that it was all a matter of money. Stokowski *is* on record as saying he thought he should be paid as much as Charlie Chaplin, Jack Dempsey or Babe Ruth. "I am an entertainer too," he said. "Why should I receive less?" And with that the "entertainer" headed for the door and Hollywood where he might hope to receive what he was worth.

Stokowski certainly believed strongly in his own relative value, but a dispute over money was only a part of the problem in Philadelphia which centered on a conflict between Stokowski's need for new challenges and the financial constraints of the Depression years. For the Philadelphia Orchestra, this was a time for consolidation rather than expansion. Stokowski, however, was simply not the sort of man to preside over routine. The series of opera and ballet performances he conducted in the late 1920s and early 1930s had been challenging and rewarding for him but they came to an abrupt halt when the money ran out. The transcontinental tour in 1936, another "first", was the realization of a Stokowski dream, but there were no more tours in sight. In fact, there was nothing new in sight for Stokowski and his orchestra at that time. It must be remembered that conductors in those days were heavily committed to their orchestras in terms of time. Whereas today conductors are with their orchestras for only about half the concert season, Stokowski, Koussevitsky and the others were expected to be there week in and week out. A guest conductor was a rare bird. Stokowski simply could not travel and make movies as well as have the orchestra. It is an indication of how badly the board wanted Stokowski to stay that they took the unprecedented step of offering him both the orchestra and his freedom when he insisted, with Eugene Ormandy stepping into the breach to take over many of the concerts in Stokowski's absence. It was then Stokowski discovered that an absent Music Director ceases to be a Music Director at all. Somebody else had to make decisions while he was away, and those decisions gradually diminished Stokowski's power. Unable to adjust to the loss of authority which he had held so long, he broke with the orchestra entirely in 1940, making it clear he had no further wish to be associated with the organization and resisted all offers to return until 1960.

3
From Philadelphia to Hollywood

To understand more fully why Stokowski would leave a magnificent orchestra of his own creation and a situation in which he had almost supreme power, to make movies, one must go back to 1932 when Stokowski was approached by Hollywood to compose a score for a movie starring John Barrymore and Katherine Hepburn. Although he had not written any original music since his organist and choirmaster days, someone had the notion that Stokowski probably knew what kind of music would be suitable for films. His concerts were often like dramatic events with musical accompaniment. The lighting, the gestures, the seating of the orchestra, the exits and entrances, the script and the acting, the little talks from the podium — all contributed to the effect and all were produced and directed in the Academy of Music by Stokowski. But more importantly, Stokowski had shown that he could reach people, particularly people who knew nothing about classical music. Stokowski was very much aware of the value of publicity and charisma.

Stokowski did not bite in 1932 for the Barrymore-Hepburn film but the offer certainly turned his head.

39

Hollywood came to symbolize for him the marriage of technology and entertainment. Stokowski had been one of the first serious musicians to attempt transcontinental radio broadcasts, and he quickly realized the potential of films. In the Academy of Music in Philadelphia Stokowski and his orchestra could play to perhaps 3,000 people at a time. On film they could play to millions.

As his final flourish as Music Director of the Philadelphia Orchestra, Stokowski made a coast to coast tour in 1936 with two concerts in Hollywood as the high point. The tour itself was one of Stokowski's dreams, and in the words of one musician, the whole orchestra was "punchdrunk with excitement." But the Hollywood concerts obviously meant something special to Stokowski, who, before the first, called the men together and told them "this must be the best." Stokowski was out to prove something; to show that he belonged there. The concert was a sensation, with Stokowski playing the music he was best known for: Bach's Toccata and Fugue in D minor in his own transcription, music from Wagner's *Tristan und Isolde* and Brahms' Symphony No. 1, this last a work he had conducted at his 1912 debut concert in Philadelphia.

Stokowski's next Hollywood offer was to take the lead role in the *Life of Wagner*. He declined. But he did appear in a film called *The Big Broadcast* in 1936 conducting Bach's Fugue in G minor. More the incorporation of a performance by a symphony and its conductor into a Hollywood film than an acting assignment, it was a breakthrough and whetted Stokowski's appetite for more. The very next year he branched further afield and appeared in *100 Men and a Girl* with young Deanna Durbin. This movie was the brainchild of German director Henry Koster, who saw Stokowski's potential as a movie star and persuaded Universal Pictures to take the plunge. From the studio's point of view it was a big risk.

40

They were not about to try to ram classical music down the throats of their customers. But the pill was considerably sugared by the film's fun and silliness and the music never held up the picture for long. The movie, about a little girl who tries to find a conductor to help unemployed musicians, pits the winning charm of fifteen-year-old Deanna Durbin against the Olympian white-haired figure of Stokowski. Much of the film is taken up with her attempts to persuade Stokowski to conduct her father's orchestra, which needs a man of Stokowski's talent and prestige to survive. In the film Stokowski is seen conducting several works including the *Hungarian* Rhapsody No. 2 by Liszt, the *Hungarian* March by Berlioz and the *Alleluia* from *Exsultate Jubilate* by Mozart, this last much against the protests of the film studio executives. In the end it proved to be one of the highlights of the film. The music for *100 Men and a Girl* was played by the Philadelphia Orchestra but what appears on the screen is quite a different ensemble, including all sorts of Hollywood actors, most notably Adolph Menjou as Deanna's father in the trombone section. Stokowski comes across as an appalling actor, stiff and arrogant even beyond the demands of his role. He may have thought he was advancing the cause of serious music, but probably achieved just the opposite result by confirming most people's suspicion that classical musicians are insufferable snobs. All in all, at least artistically, the film is second-rate at best, a thin story line badly acted and directed. Nonetheless it was a substantial commercial success saving Universal from bankruptcy and, in spite of Stokowski's performance, substantially increasing his record sales.

Stokowski's next Hollywood venture was to prove far more successful artistically as well as commercially. It was one of the most original and important films of all time: *Fantasia*. Originating as an idea of Walt Disney's to make a short cartoon feature using the music of Dukas' *The Sorcerer's Apprentice*, a much grander scheme was conceived to create a feature-length film using many different pieces and incorporating shots of Stokowski as well. The film became a landmark for the imaginative use of cartoons, and also a way of communicating great music to young people.

Fantasia, or Fanta-SI-a as Stokowski, like a German musicologist, insisted on pronouncing it, was begun in 1937 and released in 1940 as a film of such technical sophistication that it could only be shown in theatres especially prepared for it. It took four days to set up the sound system required. There were speakers positioned all around the theatre and they had to be operated manually. When the film was originally shown, the *Ave Maria* sequence at the end came from the rear of the auditorium. *Fantasia* was a frightfully expensive project and it hit the theatres at the least propitious time. It was wartime and the public response was far less than had been anticipated. Among its critics were those who had always found Stokowski's pretensions to music education unconvincing:

> This act of Stokowski's, in which he brings to the many what has been jealously withheld from them by the privileged few, was phoney even 10 years ago when with four one-hour broadcasts spread over months he first brought the beauty and inspiration of music to those who had been hearing Toscanini's two-hour broadcasts with the New York Philharmonic every Sunday. (B.H. Haggin, *The Nation*, January 11, 1941)

But the film has been revived several times since and distributed, without the elaborate technical paraphernalia, to great acclaim. It is now a classic and has paid back the original investment several times over.

A triumph of the imaginative wedding of music and moving pictures, *Fantasia* was also far ahead of its time purely in terms of sound quality. The music was recorded on film using seven or eight channels of sound from the orchestra. Then it was mixed down to three program tracks and one control track. Through careful mixing supervised by Stokowski after the original recording, individual instruments or sections of the orchestra could be highlighted, and separation could be achieved simulating modern stereo sound — 15 years before real stereo appeared!

Fantasia consists of more or less complete performances of a series of familiar symphonic masterpieces, from Bach's Toccata and Fugue in D minor to Mussorgsky's *Night on Bare Mountain*, by way of Stravinsky's *Le Sacre du Printemps* and Beethoven's *Pastoral* Symphony. For each of these pieces, Disney has provided a visual counterpart, the most famous being Dukas' *The Sorcerer's Apprentice* with Mickey Mouse in the leading role.

The film opens with the musicians of the Philadelphia Orchestra coming on stage and tuning up. Then Deems Taylor appears as master of ceremonies to introduce each piece. Finally, Stokowski mounts the podium and begins conducting his own orchestration of Bach's Toccata and Fugue in D minor. The first part of the performance contains interesting shots of the players, often ingeniously lit to underline the flow of the music. Then, as the Fugue begins, the film cuts away from the orchestra to a progression of dazzling abstract patterns related to the flow of the music. Initially resembling violin bows, the shapes gradually assume more uncertain identities, bearing a close relation to the rhythmic and dramatic contours of Bach's music throughout the sequence.

Music from Tchaikovsky's ballet the *Nutcracker* follows, and here Disney moves from abstract forms to the personification of all sorts of natural phenomena. None of it has anything to do with the original *Nutcracker* story but it is done so imaginatively one can hardly complain. Particularly memorable is the Chinese Dance in which mushrooms come to life complete with coolie hats and long robes. And who can forget the excitement and beauty of the Russian Dance, as the screen seems to overflow with dancers, orchids and thistles become Cossacks and peasant girls, moving to the magnificent playing of the Philadelphia Orchestra under Stokowski.

The fine quality of sound in *Fantasia* is particularly obvious in Dukas' *The Sorcerer's Apprentice* with its brilliant orchestration and huge climaxes. On the screen for this sequence Disney makes use of his most famous creation, Mickey Mouse. Mickey, as the Sorcerer's assistant, has the onerous task of carting pails of water endlessly up and down stairs. When the magician leaves, Mickey decides to try a short cut and save himself all that work. He dons the boss's hat and casts a spell over a broom. It works. The broom leaps into action and begins carrying the water. Mickey's problems are solved. But not so fast. He doesn't know how to stop the broom, and before long the whole place is awash with water. Mickey tries to destroy the renegade broom by chopping it up with an axe. Success. But after a moment's peace, lo and behold, each of the splinters has become a water carrier in its own right, so that there is not one, but whole battalions of them. Mickey himself is washed away in the flood. Finally, the sorcerer returns and with a wave of his hand removes the water. The sequence ends with a flourish as the Sorcerer gives his mischievous apprentice a swift kick where it will do the most good.

This whole episode is so entertaining one tends to forget that it was designed to fit the music already written. It does so perfectly. Not a note has been changed in Dukas' piece. The danger is, perhaps, that one may never hear the music again at a concert without

44

imagining Mickey Mouse, his brooms and the rampaging waters.

One of the most ambitious and frightening sequences in *Fantasia* is based on Stravinsky's ballet score, *Le Sacre du Printemps*. To this music Disney has provided a cartoon drama about the beginning of life on earth. The elemental power of the music serves as a background for volcanic eruptions, searing droughts and battles to the death between dinosaurs, images so terrifying one wonders whether this film is really intended for children. Stravinsky was not altogether happy with the Disney-Stokowski treatment of his music. When he was first approached for permission it was made clear to him that this Russian score was not copyrighted in the United States and so could be used anyway, without either permission or fee. Stravinsky contended that he never agreed to cuts in his score, nor did he approve the finished version as it was used in the film. But Walt Disney himself, in a letter to *Saturday Review* (Jan. 30, 1960), claimed Stravinsky did agree to "certain cuts and arrangements." Stravinsky has written this outraged account of his first viewing of *Fantasia*:

> The instrumentation had been improved by such stunts as having the horns play their *glissandi* an octave higher in the *Danse de la Terre*. The order of the pieces had been shuffled, and the most difficult of them eliminated — though this did not save the musical performance, which was execrable. I will say nothing about the visual complement as I do not wish to criticize an unresisting imbecility. (Igor Stravinsky and Robert Craft, *Expositions and Developments*. London: Faber and Faber, 1962, pp. 145-146)

The most astonishing thing about *Fantasia* is that a long piece by Stravinsky could have been used at all for a children's entertainment in 1940. Disney and Stokowski cannot be accused of giving the kids nothing but pablum. There is a real musical and emotional challenge in this sequence. Again, it must be pointed out that the performance of the music stands on its own quite well. Stokowski does romanticize Stravinsky's score here and there, but for the most part he and his orchestra do it justice. Stokowski had recorded *Le Sacre du Printemps* with the Philadelphia Orchestra in 1928 but, of course, the sound is not all it ought to be, considering the nature of the score, with its brilliant range of colours and its extreme dynamic range. The 1939 recording made for *Fantasia* is far more vivid.

For many who have seen *Fantasia*, the finest sequence in the film is the *Pastoral* Symphony. Nearly the whole of Beethoven's Sixth Symphony is represented on the screen as an idyllic scene on the slopes of Mount Olympus, with unicorns, the winged horse Pegasus, Bacchus the God of wine, centaurs, (creatures part human and part horse) and centaurettes. The Disney cartoonists outdid themselves for the *Pastoral* Symphony with images of the utmost beauty, laced with a gentle humour. Naturally, the bucolic scene does have its darker moments as required by the thunderstorm in the fourth movement of Beethoven's Symphony. And here Disney has worked wonders. In spite of itself, the audience is intensely concerned about the fate of the young fauns caught in the storm, and shrinks back as they do at the sight of Zeus up in the clouds hurling thunderbolts to the crash of timpani. But finally Zeus tires, and pulling a cloud up around himself, inadvertently dropping a few more thunderbolts as he does so, goes to sleep. Once again the images devised by Disney and his men could not have been better suited to the music.

Stokowski recorded the *Pastoral* Symphony again in 1954 but the *Fantasia* version is quite fine in its own right. Since the later one is with the NBC Symphony, the earlier version remains an important documentation of Stokowski's Beethoven performances with the Philadelphia Orchestra. The string playing is quite incomparable. The general conception is romantic with lush tone, opulent phrasing and excessively slow tempos in the slower movements. The second movement in particular is more *adagio* than *andante molto mosso* as indicated in the score, but in the 1954 NBC Symphony recording Stokowski again takes much the same tempo.

For Ponchielli's *Dance of the Hours* from the opera *La Gioconda*, Disney and his cartoonists have created animal ballets by the most unlikely creatures imaginable. The whole sequence, a complete send-up of classical ballet with elephants, ostriches, rhinos and alligators flitting about in tutus, seems more grotesque than funny. Perhaps the Disney crew disliked the music.

In the final part of *Fantasia*, Disney and Stokowski joined together Mussorgsky's *Night on Bare Mountain* and Schubert's *Ave Maria* in a version for chorus and orchestra. The *Bare Mountain* music is represented on the screen by a most ghoulish sort of Witches' Sabbath presided over by a horrifying Devil figure. As the *Bare Mountain* music subsides and the Schubert music creeps in, a procession of monks, supposedly symbolizing the triumph of life and hope over despair and death, and providing a sort of apotheosis for the film, appears on the screen. *Fantasia* does not really have any theme as all beyond an attempt to interest young people in great music, using the technology of film and the imagination of gifted illustrators. To tack a message on at the end seems somehow contrived and unnecessary.

Fantasia was both a triumph and a failure depending on one's perspective. At the time, it was an innovative and fulfilling experience for those who worked on it. Stokowski's collaboration with Walt Disney produced one of the most beautiful motion pictures ever made. The cost was so great, however, and the return so uncertain, that no plans were made to attempt another like it so that *Fantasia* was a kind of dead end for

Stokowski. But being a man of infinite resourcefulness and unwilling to rest on his laurels, he soon came up with another project which, like *Fantasia*, was decidedly offbeat for a conductor of his stature. He set out to found a youth orchestra, not just any youth orchestra, but a youth orchestra to end all youth orchestras.

In 1940, from his Hollywood home, Stokowski announced that the new orchestra would soon be formed. After weeks of intensive rehearsals, it would then make a tour of South America. Players between the ages of 18 and 25 would be drawn from every state in the Union and standards would equal the Philadelphia Orchestra's. There were those who thought Stokowski had surely gone mad this time, but like so many Stokowski dreams, this one too became a reality. Stokowski was not alone in his enthusiasm for the idea. The American State Department saw a tour by the cream of American youth as excellent propaganda at a time when war was raging in Europe and the United States wished to maintain a good relationship with the still largely neutral South American countries. Unfortunately, the State Department was unable to find any money for the operation of the orchestra. This part of it was up to Stokowski. Having recorded exclusively for RCA Victor since he began his recording career in 1917, Stokowski decided to approach the head of RCA, General Sarnoff. But at that time Sarnoff was heavily committed to Toscanini and the NBC Symphony, and RCA decided to send them to South America instead. Being a man of considerable determination, Stokowski went straight to RCA's biggest competitor, Columbia Records, and made the same request. Columbia was very interested in the project, probably hoping that it might be the means for weaning Stokowski away from RCA for good, and agreed, therefore, to underwrite the entire cost of the South American tour in return for exclusive recordings of the new orchestra.

Rehearsals began in June, 1940 in Atlantic City and the first concert was given July 21. The program included three Stokowski staples: the Bach, G minor Fugue, the Brahms First Symphony and the *Prelude and Liebestod* from *Tristan* by Wagner. This was no ordinary youth orchestra. Its players were certainly young, but they were entirely qualified to sit in professional orchestras. As good as his word, Stokowski came up with players who could have made it into the Philadelphia Orchestra if there had been a vacancy, and, in fact, many of them did go on to join major orchestras. The principal flute of the All-American Youth Orchestra was Albert Tipton, later of the Detroit Symphony; the principal oboe was Harold Gomberg who still holds that post with the New York Philharmonic; the principal clarinettist was Robert McInnes, later of the San Francisco Symphony; the first bassoonist was Manuel Zegler, also still a principal in the New York Philharmonic; the horn section included Ed Murphy, later a member of the St. Louis Symphony and James Chambers, who became a member of the New York Philharmonic and is now its personnel manager. Finally, the concertmaster was Paul Schure who was to hold the same position with the Los Angeles Philharmonic. It was an all-star cast if ever there was one. Yet it must be remembered that these young players, just beginning their professional careers, were not then stars. It is further evidence of Stokowski's amazing ability to build an orchestra.

As the orchestra was initially formed for the purpose of making a South American tour, in an inspired public relations gesture for the sake of the war effort, they sailed to Rio shortly after the Atlantic City concert. One of the highlights of the tour was a concert in Montevideo. But it was memorable for a variety of non-musical reasons. The concert program listed the con-

49

ductor as Leonard Stokes, and Stokowski getting wind of this, refused to go on. The audience began to grow increasingly restless as the assistant conductor, Saul Caston, pleaded with Stokowski in his dressing room. But Stokowski was adamant. "Saul, you conduct," was his only response. Finally, after Stokowski had been assured that all the offensive programs had been collected and taken out of circulation, he agreed to go on stage. However, the evening's excitement was not over. In the middle of a Bach Fugue, Stokowski, becoming annoyed with a man taking pictures from a third tier box, left the podium, went up to the box and started hitting the man. Apparently this had the desired effect, and Stokowski returned to the podium to resume conducting. It was quite an evening.

This South American tour by the All-American Youth Orchestra was such a great success, that plans were made to continue its operation. But many of the younger members of the orchestra joined the Armed Forces and the character of the ensemble began to change with the incorporation of older players, including some from the Philadelphia Orchestra. After the South American tour the orchestra became known simply as the All-American Orchestra.

Although the Columbia engineers had accompanied Stokowski and the orchestra to South America in 1940, all they came back with were several recordings of Brazilian folk music supervised, according to a note on the ensuing album, by Stokowski. The first recordings of the orchestra were made in California just after the tour. With the All-American Youth Orchestra and later the All-American Orchestra, Stokowski recorded a great deal of music that he had already recorded once or even twice with the Philadelphia Orchestra for RCA. Columbia Records recorded the All-American in order to compete with RCA for the Stokowski market. These included recordings of Dvorak's *New World* Symphony, Mussorgsky's *Pictures at an Exhibition*, Schubert's *Unfinished* Symphony and many Bach transcriptions. Stokowski did record one piece for the first time: Ravel's *Bolero*. Given the popularity of the piece, it is rather surprising that he has never recorded it again. Stokowski gave one of the first American performances of the work and has played it many times since. However, his recording of *Bolero* is a disappointment, considering the nature of the piece and Stokowski's flair for showpieces of this sort. It does not rise to much of a climax and Stokowski does little to maintain interest and tension. He does make some alterations in the score, leaving out grace notes and substituting a clarinet for a soprano saxophone, but these make the work even less interesting.

Stokowski's interest in new music led him to play and record several contemporary works with the All-American Orchestra. One of them was a suite called *Tales from our Countryside* by the American Henry Cowell, a composer whose music Stokowski has always championed. The recording features the composer himself at the piano.

Due to the success of the South American tour, the orchestra was reconstituted for the following summer. This time it toured coast to coast in the United States and made more recordings, the last on July 21, 1941, just prior to the disbanding of the ensemble. In spite of the good impression it had made on everyone who had heard it, the orchestra was allowed to die after only two seasons due to lack of funds. The time was simply not right. By the summer of 1941 the United States was heavily involved in the Second World War and the situation was deteriorating. Columbia Records had paid the cost of the South American tour as well as the American tour the next year, but, having by 1941 made all the recordings they could possibly market with the orchestra for the time being, they withdrew their support. There were no other sponsors waiting in the wings.

Characteristically, Stokowski wasted no time getting involved in other activities. Even while he was in charge of the All-American, which functioned only in the summer, he guest conducted extensively and continued his annual appearances with the Philadelphia Orchestra. Within a few months of the completion of his work with the All-American in 1941, he was invited to become co-conductor of the NBC Symphony. Early that same year, Toscanini had submitted his near-annual resignation and there was some fear that he really meant it this time. Stokowski was engaged as an insurance policy, and if need be, he could succeed Toscanini as sole conductor of the NBC Symphony. But it did not work out that way. The co-conductor arrangement survived only one season. Toscanini complained that Stokowski was ruining his orchestra, asking for a different sound, taking all sorts of liberties with the music and even reseating the players. Recalling what had happened when Toscanini exchanged podiums with Stokowski in 1930, surely someone could have foreseen trouble. With the exception of concertmaster Misha Mishakoff, Stokowski got along with most of the players in the NBC Symphony better than he had with Toscanini's New York Philharmonic. Mishakoff admitted that Stokowski made the orchestra sound gorgeous but he could not accept Stokowski's lack of respect for the printed score — removing two bars here and two bars there as the mood took him. Toscanini, of course, was famous for his absolute fidelity to what the composer wrote. For his part, Stokowski managed to get off a few remarks of his own about Toscanini. "Some conductors insult the players and call them peculiar Italian names, but," Stokowski added enigmatically, "that is not what makes them great."

Among the works Stokowski conducted with the NBC Symphony was the American première of Prokofiev's cantata, *Alexander Nevsky*. Stokowski did not record the work with the NBC but he did record excerpts from Prokofiev's opera *Love for Three Oranges*. Another Russian piece Stokowski recorded with the orchestra was one of his perennial favourites, the *Russian Easter* Overture by Rimsky-Korsakov, perhaps one of the more vulgar and empty potboilers by any composer of reputation. Stokowski, however, has recorded the work many times over, obviously seeing in it something that escapes many others entirely. For the NBC recording he made some unique alterations in the score, the most obvious of which is the use of a bass soloist although none is indicated in the score. The performance is a very good one, with as much hysteria and aggressiveness as any Toscanini performance and far more awareness of orchestral colour.

One of the recording anomalies of Stokowski's NBC Symphony career was the *Arioso* by Bach in that Stokowski had recorded the same work with the All-American Orchestra in July 1941, just four months previous. But here again, it was probably a matter of competition between the record companies — RCA Victor with the NBC Symphony and Columbia with the All-American. In any case, there is not much to choose between the two performances; both reflect the sumptuous Stokowski string tone at its best, or at its worst if one does not happen to think this style of playing is appropriate to Bach. The NBC recording is not immediately recognizable as the work of a more experienced professional orchestra, although at the time it was reputed to be the best in the world. This is perhaps another illustration of Stokowski's uncanny ability to get

53

the best from his musicians, even when, as in the case of the All-American Orchestra, the players have been together only a very short time.

A good orchestra is a number of wonderful players with good instruments in their hands, playing in a good hall with a good conductor. Whether they've played together before or not is much less important than most people think. (Stokowski)

After his brief association with the NBC Symphony Stokowski founded yet another orchestra. This time it was not a youth orchestra but a rather unique ensemble nevertheless. In 1944 Mayor La Guardia of New York City invited some 15 citizens to form a committee to discuss possible uses for the old Mecca Temple. The committee came up with the idea of converting the building into an Arts Centre, a forerunner of Lincoln Centre, only on a much smaller, less expensive scale, and with the purpose of being more fully accessible to the average person. This plan was approved and the New York City Centre was created to house artistic ventures of all kinds. Invited to form a resident orchestra for the new Centre, Stokowski accepted and became the first well-known musician to get involved in the project. Without accepting a fee of any kind due to the Centre's meagre budget, Stokowski not only conducted the orchestra, he also spent time arranging for concerts, recordings, lighting and even the printing of the programs, as well as designing a new acoustical shell for the Centre. At Christmas, Stokowski put in money of his own for a pageant.

It almost goes without saying, in light of Stokowski's career up to this point, that he put together a crack orchestra for the City Centre. Within a matter of weeks, the orchestra was unmistakably his, capable of great brilliance and virtuosity and a wide range of tone colours. The exciting and beautiful recording of excerpts from Bizet's *Carmen*, which includes purely orchestral arrangements of some of the arias, is a good example of Stokowski's achievement with the New York City Symphony. On December 10, 1944 they also recorded the tone poem *Death and Transfiguration* by Richard Strauss, a favourite of Stokowski's which he has recorded several times. He has a real flair for programmatic music of this kind. One of the musicians in the Philadelphia Orchestra recalled that when Stokowski began a performance of this work a look of death came over his face mirroring the agony of the dying man which Strauss tried to express in the music. Such a dramatic touch on Stokowski's part was just what the orchestra needed to get into the spirit of the piece. In this recording Stokowski makes a curious alteration in the score, which is all too typical of his tendency as a conductor to underline the obvious to ensure the listener does not miss it. Near the very end of the piece Stokowski has the trumpets play a little louder than the *pianissimo* indicated in the score. The phrase the trumpets play then becomes a clear imitation of what the violins have just played — a three-note descending figure, indicating a farewell to life. (This same figure had been used by Beethoven in his Piano Sonata *Les Adieux* to denote a less permanent kind of departure.) Usually, the trumpets play so softly in this passage they are barely audible. But not in Stokowski's performance, and in making this alteration, Stokowski has, perhaps, destroyed the ethereal beauty of the passage.

A small point, but indicative of the sort of thing Stokowski does as a matter of course. He treats the score as a sketch. If an effect indicated in the score just does not "sound" in performance, then he feels justified in making sure it does. Reasoning that the composer knew what he wanted but could not always express it in notes on paper, Stokowski believes it is up to someone far

55

more expert in matters of performance, *i.e.* a conductor like himself, to change the notes to the extent necessary to realize the composer's intentions. One of the problems with an argument of this sort, however, is that it rests on an assumption that there is a better way of determining a composer's intention than looking at what he wrote in the score. That is a very dubious assumption. Furthermore, it is often a personal judgement as to what "sounds" and what does not in performance. If, for example, one believes that Strauss wanted the trumpets in *Death and Transfiguration* to be little more than a whisper or echo of the violins, Stokowski has violated the composer's intentions by having them play louder. In this case, greater clarity would not be an improvement.

As he could not afford to conduct without fee indefinitely, Stokowski stayed only one season with the New York City Symphony. His concerts with this orchestra were typically exciting and unusual and on one occasion, Tommy Dorsey was invited to play a trombone concerto. Without the time to devote exclusively to even a worthwhile project such as this one, Stokowski left and was succeeded by the young Leonard Bernstein, who continued to develop the orchestra and, like his predecessor, made contemporary music an outstanding feature of its programming.

Stokowski left New York to return to Hollywood and take the reins of the Hollywood Bowl Orchestra. One of the first outdoor acoustical shells, with seating for a huge audience of about 20,000, the Bowl had been in existence for years and had become the most famous concert site of its kind. Stokowski arrived with a three-year contract taking many of the young City Centre players with him. Again, true to form, he transformed the orchestra beyond recognition. One of the most curious recordings Stokowski made with the Hollywood

Bowl Orchestra was his own arrangement of the *Hungarian* Dance No. 1 by Brahms. Stokowski's version is so strange one begins to suspect that it was intended as a joke.

In spite of Stokowski's three-year contract in Hollywood, he stayed only about a year and a half and then returned to New York. While in Hollywood, Stokowski enlivened the Bowl's concert seasons with his usual blend of the familiar, the bizarre and the brand-new. On Veteran's Night he accompanied Frank Sinatra in "Ol' Man River;" on other occasions he conducted opera at the Bowl in fully staged productions, among the most memorable of which was a *Carmen* complete with real horses on stage. But Stokowski did not stay long enough to make the sort of impact he had made in Philadelphia. In fact, after his resignation from the Philadelphia Orchestra in 1936, he did not remain anywhere for very long. He was a man without an orchestra searching for something he perhaps never really succeeded in actually finding or even recognizing. That, it seems, is the tragedy of Stokowski. He enjoyed innumerable triumphs after Philadelphia, and whatever orchestra he conducted became almost instantly his. Yet he never rested long enough in any one place to have a real effect on the way things were done. He was like a shooting star, shining brightly but constantly moving on. Even while he was conductor of the Philadelphia Orchestra, Stokowski had his eye on a permanent post with an orchestra in New York, and after his brief sojourn with the Hollywood Bowl Orchestra he looked there again. More correctly, New York looked to him and Stokowski appeared for all the world like the next conductor of the New York Philharmonic. After years of moving from place to place Stokowski wanted very much to settle down once more, and the Philharmonic seemed to provide the best possible reason for doing so.

4
New York Revisited

Stokowski's abrupt exit from Hollywood in late 1946 was attributed by some to his wife, Gloria Vanderbilt, wanting to resume her acting career in New York. But there was a more compelling reason. The post of Music Director of the New York Philharmonic had just become vacant with the sudden departure of Artur Rodzinski, and the management turned to Stokowski in desperation. Over the next several seasons Stokowski conducted more of the Philharmonic's concerts than anyone else and it appeared he had the inside track for the permanent post. However, he did not get it. Dimitri Mitropoulos was chosen instead for reasons which are not altogether clear.

The New York Philharmonic had gone through an uncertain period after Toscanini's resignation in 1936. His immediate successor, Sir John Barbirolli, was virtually run out of town by the orchestra and the critics. Under Barbirolli's successor, Artur Rodzinski, who had been Stokowski's assistant for several years in Philadelphia, the New York Philharmonic seemed about to pull itself together and recover from its post-Toscanini depression. But like Stokowski, Rodzinski was both an individualist and an unpredictable eccentric. He had a reputation for breaking contracts as often as he honoured them. In the middle of the New York Philharmonic's 1946-47 season Rodzinski resigned, charging that the orchestra's manager Arthur Judson, who also happened to be the head of Columbia Artist's Management, was using the orchestra to promote the careers of artists managed by Columbia, a practice Rodzinski regarded as not only a conflict of interest but also an infringement on his perogatives as Music Director. The Philharmonic board tried to pacify Rodzinski by offering him a three-year contract and a raise in salary, but the volatile conductor preferred to wash his hands of the whole mess and most especially of Arthur Judson. Rodzinski quit the New York Philharmonic on February 3, 1947 and went on to conduct the Chicago Symphony, but was fired just a year later for alleged disorganization and irresponsibility. In spite of Rodzinski's notorious irascibility, there was some truth in his charges concerning Judson. These were regularly revived by the press and finally forced Judson's removal nine years later.

Coincidentally, Judson had been the manager of the Philadelphia Orchestra during the great Stokowski years from 1915 to 1935. Judson had always admired Stokowski, but they too had had their differences. During the period of Stokowski's first resignation in Philadelphia, Judson, as one of his opponents, had been forced out. But the manager knew a charismatic figure when he saw one and invited Stokowski to fill in for Rodzinski in the chaotic Philharmonic season of 1946-47. Taking over most of Rodzinski's schedule, Stokowski conducted 33 New York Philharmonic concerts that season in addition to 11 concerts on the spring tour. The next year he conducted 33 more and the following year, no less than 51. During these years Bruno Walter held the title of Musical Adviser, but as his musical tastes were too conservative, he was not seriously considered for the post of Music Director. Nonetheless, as the titular head of the orchestra, it was more or less expected that he conduct most of the Philharmonic's concerts, something which, in fact, Stokowski did. The race for the permanent post was narrowed to Stokowski, Charles Munch and Dimitri Mitropoulos, with Stokowski, as its *de facto* conductor, seemingly in the lead. Munch fell out of the running when he was appointed to head the Boston Symphony in 1949, and finally the board chose Mitropoulos over Stokowski.

Circumstances going back to the days of the keen rivalry which existed between the Philadelphia orchestra under Stokowski and the New York Philharmonic directed by Toscanini may have been instrumental in Stokowski's failure to secure the position. As has already been recounted, the two conductors exchanged podiums in 1930, during which time the New York Philharmonic harboured a dislike of Stokowski which never entirely disappeared. From then on, Stokowski's relationship with the orchestra was correct rather than enthusiastic. On the other hand, a certain reluctance on the part of Judson and his board to invite trouble by appointing a man as mercurial, impractical and strong-minded as Stokowski, however brilliant he might be, could have prompted the decision. In the board's view, Dimitri Mitropoulos would be a more co-operative Music Director. As things turned out, he was, but had little else to offer. The orchestra's ensemble and discipline almost disappeared, there was no consistency in the programming and as a result, audiences declined drastically. The Philharmonic began to recover only with the appointment of Leonard Bernstein in 1957. In retrospect it looks like a monumental blunder was made. Stokowski was available and, given the chance, just might have worked wonders with the Philharmonic.

Stokowski and Mitropoulos co-conducted the New York Philharmonic for the 1949-50 season, but the next season, following Mitropoulos' appointment, Stokowski did not appear at all. In fact, he did not return to the Philharmonic until the Mitropoulos regime was over and Leonard Bernstein installed, and only then for the occasional concert. With the selection of Mitropoulos, Stokowski's deep involvement with this orchestra came to an end.

On some of the recordings Stokowski made for Columbia with the New York Philharmonic between 1947 and 1949, he achieved superb results. In Tchaikovsky's *Francesca da Rimini* Stokowski gives us a tremendous wash of colour and drama. He is apt to hold key notes in a melodic phrase just a little longer than the score indicates, but in this case, it is all to good effect. On January 27, 1949 Stokowski conducted the first New York performance of the Symphony No. 6 by Vaughan Williams, and recorded it with the Philharmonic about a month later.

In these same years, Stokowski recorded with another orchestra for RCA. Created for the sole purpose of making recordings, this orchestra did not exist as a permanent body nor did it give public concerts. On the albums, conductor and orchestra were identified simply as "Leopold Stokowski and his Symphony Orchestra." This was not just any pick-up orchestra, however, but a crack ensemble containing some of the best free-lance players in New York as well as musicians from the New York Philharmonic. Stokowski made a vast number of recordings with "his Symphony Orchestra," achieving incredible results considering the impermanence of the ensemble. Among the best of these are Debussy's *Afternoon of a Faun* with solo flautist Julius Baker, and Sibelius' *Swan of Tuonela* with Mitch Miller playing the important english horn solo. One of the most interesting, however, is Stravinsky's *Firebird* Suite from 1950. In the last movement of this piece the tremolo strings build to a *crescendo* followed by the full orchestra coming in with *forte* repeated notes in 7/4 time. But at the beginning of each 7/4 bar there is a *glissando* or slide in the horns marked *fortissimo* which is almost never heard clearly, if at all. It is even obscured in the composer's own recording

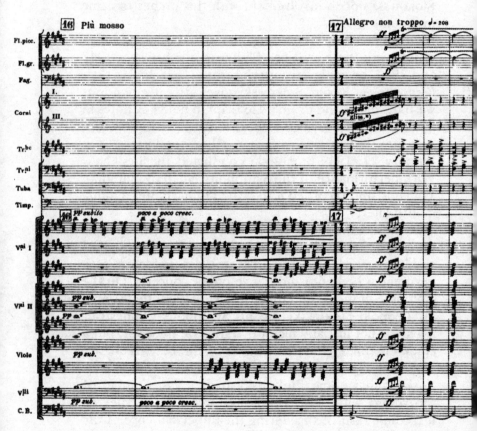

by a timpani stroke. In an effort to bring out the *glissando*, Stokowski had the horns play it more slowly, and to make sure no one could possibly miss this, he supplied them with their own microphone. A resourceful touch on Stokowski's part but, characteristically, one that went too far. Playing the *glissando* more slowly necessarily distorts the rhythm of the music as a whole, and the extra microphone creates a very phoney effect. Stokowski must have had misgivings because he returned the horn *glissando* to its former obscurity when he recorded the work again later with the Berlin Philharmonic.

Throughout the 1950s Stokowski was one of the world's most popular conductors. He was in great demand to lead all the major orchestras and his records sold even better than Toscanini's. To those who knew him only on records, Stokowski, busy exploring the pop concert repertoire, was apt to appear less serious and more superficial than Toscanini who was recording Beethoven symphonies, Brahms symphonies and complete operas. Such different repertoires, however, were not surprising since both conductors were under contract to the same company, RCA Victor, who made sure its two star conductors did not compete with each other.

Nonetheless, it would be a mistake to compare these conductors solely on the basis of the recordings they made. In his later years Toscanini, true to the tradition of most older conductors, had a small repertoire which he liked to rework over and over again. He had an almost complete indifference to contemporary music. Stokowski, on the other hand, has a huge ever-changing repertoire and avoids repeating the same works, while continuing to present first performances of works by living composers. At every stage in his career Stokowski has been a pioneer, an advocate of new music and has persisted in spite of resistance from his employer, his board or his audiences. In musical circles this has caused

63

no end of annoyance. Stokowski's reputation as a man who can be counted on to turn up with a program containing difficult works, got him into trouble in Philadelphia, at NBC, and later in Houston. Stokowski is rather unique in that for the record-buying public he is a popularizer, somehow making familiar music sound fresh and important all over again, and for the concert-going public he is the champion of new music, presenting pieces that might well fail in the hands of a lesser conductor.

Sir Thomas Beecham was another conductor who could breathe new life into old warhorses and it is worth while trying to discover just what these conductors did to make the music sound so much better. In the first place, as personalities and technicians, such men are able to enhance anything an orchestra plays. In the case of Beecham this was achieved by sheer bravado and panache. For Stokowski, it is, perhaps, more a technical thing — an ability to hear what an orchestra is doing, to make corrections and adjust balances, and overall, a special talent for rehearsing that makes the players want to improve so that more is accomplished in a few hours than most conductors get done in a week. The interpretative skill possessed by both Beecham and Stokowski, which allows them to see in familiar music something which has escaped the eye and the ear of other conductors, is another of their secrets. Finally, they have the ability and *chuizpah* to see in the score what other conductors have failed to observe simply because it is not there; that is, they often *alter* the score to improve its effect.

A concert staple such as Rimsky-Korsakov's *Scheherazade* is an excellent piece for illustrating the foregoing. Most audiences have heard it so many times that their interest in it has been all but destroyed by repetition and lack-lustre performances. Stokowski's

1951 recording of the work with the Philharmonia Orchestra reminds us that *Scheherazade* is, after all, a beautiful piece and a work of genius. The performance has been prepared to the point where nothing happens by chance. No musician is in any doubt as to what he must do and Stokowski's control is absolute. *Scheherazade* exploits the various colours in the orchestra as no work had ever done before. It is full of *cadenzas* for solo violin and for most of the wind instruments. Rimsky-Korsakov also uses them in novel combinations and exploits technical features of the instruments which most composers did not even suspect existed. Stokowski is sensitive not only to the colours but also to the nuances of phrasing and the dramatic flow of the piece. This performance has a logic which binds together the work's impetus as well as the episodic nature of the movements. Stokowski's inevitable alterations in the score involve both changes in tempo and dynamics. At the beginning of the last movement, for example, the tempo marking is *allegro* and the metre is 6/8. There is an orchestral introduction after which the solo violin enters over a sustained note in the basses and cellos. Up until the violin *cadenza*, the music is to be played in tempo. Stokowski, however, begins in a very slow tempo and then speeds up. This is a typical Stokowski touch and it does enliven the music and make it more dramatic and compelling. A little further into the movement, Stokowski makes an additional adjustment. After the violin *cadenza* there is another short orchestral *tutti*, followed by another violin *cadenza*, over a pedal bass. Each time the pedal bass occurs, the composer marks it *pianissimo* in the score. The first time Stokowski plays it as such, but the second time he changes the marking to *sforzando*, so that instead of entering softly, the basses and cellos come in with a violent attack. This clearly violates the letter of the score, but not its spirit. A *sforzando* attack is logically possible here and helps to bind together the frequent breaks in the music. The music is given a thrust that leads helpfully to the increasingly urgent character of the violin *cadenza*. An interesting stroke on Stokowski's part, but few conductors would dare to do it.

Stokowski has recorded *Scheherazade* five times in his career, twice with the Philadelphia in 1927 and 1934, once with the Philharmonia in 1951, once with the New Philharmonia in 1964, and most recently, with the Royal Philharmonic in 1975. The earliest versions with the Philadelphia give a magnificent impression of what that orchestra was and what miracles Stokowski could work with it. The Philharmonia version is better still in terms of sound and as an example of Stokowski's way with the score. Formed just after the war as a recording orchestra by Walter Legge, the Philharmonia quickly became known as one of the finest anywhere, recording frequently with Karajan and Klemperer and performing under Furtwängler and Toscanini as well. A number of the Karajan recordings reveal a superb orchestra, but one neither especially colourful nor distinctive in its sound or style of playing. However, the Stokowski recording of *Scheherazade* with the Philharmonia is another story. It is impossible to know how much Stokowski might have changed the sound of the orchestra, but he certainly got every imaginable colour from it. Stokowski's 1964 and 1975 stereo recordings of *Scheherazade*, while more vividly captured by the engineers, lack spontaneity. One gets the feeling that Stokowski and the orchestras were not yet entirely comfortable with each other.

While Stokowski recorded mostly standard or even pop concert repertoire for RCA in the 1950s, from time to time he persuaded the company to become a little more adventurous. In addition to pieces by Rimsky-

Korsakov, Tchaikovsky and Saint-Saëns, Stokowski recorded works of Stravinsky, Bartok, Shostakovich, and bolder still, works by American composers including Lou Harrison, Ben Weber and Roger Goeb. Any discussion of Stokowski's recordings during the early 1950s must also include mention of excerpts from Mussorgsky's opera *Boris Godonov*, an RCA album produced in San Francisco. Stokowski has conducted only rarely in the opera house during his long career, but he loves the music of opera and plays it in concert form whenever possible. He has frequently made what he calls a synthesis of music from an opera, the best known being those from *Boris Godonov* and Wagner's *Tristan und Isolde*. In these arrangements, Stokowski has simply eliminated all the vocal parts, transferring them to instruments in the orchestra, and joined excerpts of the original score together to form a more or less logical sequence of music. In the case of *Boris*, Stokowski has recorded the synthesis several times, but has also recorded excerpts from the opera in their original form with solo voices and chorus. While Stokowski's synthesis of music from *Boris* is not at all bad, his 1954 recording of parts of the original score is a greater achievement. With Nicola Rossi-Lemeny as Boris and with the San Francisco Symphony and Opera Chorus, Stokowski makes the music exciting and compelling. He is especially successful in getting the chorus to suggest the roughness and vigour of Russian peasants. There is no room here for merely beautiful and correct singing. Stokowski concentrates on the drama and the pageantry with really marvellous results.

5
From New York to Houston

After years of wandering as a guest conductor, Stokowski unexpectedly settled down in 1955, accepting the post of Music Director of the Houston Symphony. Stokowski always did the thing least expected of him so it should have surprised no one that he would choose to take charge of a second-rate orchestra in a part of the world not noted for its cultural sophistication. A man of the world, a lover of good food and high society, Stokowski could have settled almost anywhere with almost any first-class orchestra. Why Houston, of all places?

But then why did he quit the Philadelphia Orchestra in 1936? Why did he form a youth orchestra in 1940? Why did he go to Hollywood to make films? Why did he do half the things he did? Stokowski tires very quickly of routine and by the mid-1950s, after years of recording in New York and appearing the world over with different orchestras, he was probably ready for a complete change. He needed a new challenge and Houston certainly offered that. Before Stokowski took it over, the Houston Symphony had been through a series of bad experiences with different conductors, among them

Efrem Kurtz and Ferenc Fricsay. It was rumoured in the music business that the Houston board and the manager were impossible, and that the audience was totally unsophisticated. Enter Stokowski. To show his heart was in the right place, Stokowski asked to be introduced to a real Texas cowboy, which was exactly what the locals, after years of trying to shake off the wild west image, did not want. Stokowski's next move was to offer an instant *a priori* analysis of what was wrong with musical life in Houston. The orchestra should start presenting opera, he said, in his patented Olympian tones. It was gently pointed out to the maestro that the Houston Grand Opera Association was already in existence and making use of the Houston Symphony. To cap it all, Stokowski insisted on mispronouncing the name of the city itself. For him it was "Hooston" and "Hooston" it was going to stay. All in all, not a very auspicious beginning in the heart of the American Southwest.

The Houston Symphony hired Stokowski to rebuild the orchestra and to make it one of the world's finest as quickly as possible. Plenty of money was available to do the job and all that was lacking was the right man as Music Director. With Stokowski's considerable reputation as a builder of orchestras, his prestige and his glamour, the Houston Symphony felt it would be in the news more often and might even acquire a recording contract. The Stokowski era got off to a roaring start when NBC-TV broadcast part of a Stokowski rehearsal with the orchestra even before the first concert.

Stokowski set about in his usual methodical way to reshape the Houston Symphony. Rather than fire a great many players, he was content to reseat the orchestra and try to inspire the musicians to pay more attention to instrumental colour and balance. There was one characteristic technological innovation — Stokowski

69

had an organ company build a small two-octave instrument to supplement and enhance the resonance of the double basses.

He introduced an enormous number of new works to Houston including Carl Orff's modern classic *Carmina Burana*. Stokowski apparently gave the piece a tremendous reading and recorded it soon afterwards with the same forces — the Houston Chorale and Youth Symphony Boy's Choir in addition to the Houston Symphony. A perhaps apocryphal anecdote related to the recording has it that in one spot, as the soprano soloist was unable to reach the required high D, the missing note was supplied by the baritone soloist in falsetto. Such an interpolation on the recording is undetectable, but then any competent engineer could easily disguise this sort of cheat.

The United States première of Shostakovich's Symphony No. 11, first performed just less than a year before in Russia, was another important work brought to Houston by Stokowski. Still determined at age 73 to keep his audiences abreast of new repertoire, Stokowski peppered nearly all his Houston concerts with new or unknown pieces, playing Orff, Ives, Cowell, Khatchaturian and Shostakovich his first season. However, resistance was considerable. Many listeners were bewildered, bored or irritated. Stokowski was urged to moderate his programming, and to everyone's surprise he did. The second year, Stokowski conducted 14 of the season's 20 weeks, out of which eight were devoted to a Beethoven cycle. To pacify the disgruntled subscribers still further, no advance details were given of Stokowski's programs for the other six weeks.

In the 1957-58 season the orchestra expanded from 20 to 24 weeks of concerts and Stokowski reached the end of his initial three-year contract. It was generally felt that he had done well in Houston. The orchestra was playing better than it had ever done before and Stokowski's presence had generated both revenue and audiences. He was invited to continue as Music Director of the orchestra.

Yet all was not well. Even after three years Stokowski had not taken up residence in Houston, staying only long enough for his concerts and making no attempt to get involved in the life of the community. There was no affection between himself and the members of the Houston Symphony with whom he was formal and distant. By the end of the third season general interest in Stokowski was dwindling. The glamour had worn off and audiences started to decline. When further suggestions were made to Stokowski to reduce the amount of new music in his concerts, he acquiesced yet again and announced plans for a Brahms cycle, but he had been hurt by the constant attacks on his programming. Things worsened in the 1959-60 season. The orchestra's manager, Tom Johnson, had become interested in Sir John Barbirolli and was actively seeking to bring him to Houston. Finally, the situation came to a head and Stokowski himself announced at the final concert on April 4 that he would not be continuing beyond the next season. The news that Barbirolli would succeed him in the fall of 1961 followed, which meant that Stokowski would be going through the season as a lame duck Music Director. It was not a position he was likely to enjoy and it did not last much past a few concerts. The board seemed more than happy to accept Stokowski's resignation when he sent word from New York that he had had enough.

Stokowski has always maintained that he left the Houston Symphony due to an incident involving racial prejudice. He had planned a performance of Schoenberg's massive *Gurrelieder*, a work requiring three choirs. The State University Chorus, one of those

71

engaged, objected to the participation of black people in one of the other choirs. Stokowski was unable to tolerate such prejudice. He refused to agree to the elimination of the blacks and asked to be released from his contract. In light of the premature announcement that Barbirolli would soon be taking over, this gesture, while certainly commendable, may have involved some face-saving as well.

Stokowski's recordings with the Houston Symphony are not among his most distinguished. The 1958 recording of Glière's Symphony No. 3, *Ilya Murometz*, indicates that after about three years in Houston some of the Stokowski flair for orchestral colour had been imposed on the orchestra, but there is also a certain coolness in the playing and conducting. His 1940 recording of the work with the Philadelphia Orchestra achieves a great deal more verve and brilliance in comparison to the Houston recording which, while clearer, is not nearly so exciting. The playing is very ordinary and Stokowski's tempos are far too deliberate for the nature of the music in the later version.

Stokowski was never one to concentrate his energies in any one place or project. While he was withdrawing from Houston he was active as a guest conductor all over the world, including Moscow where he made a record of Prokofiev's Symphony No. 5. His most important new activity was with the New York City Opera. Stokowski had never conducted much opera in his career, and for the very first time he worked regularly in an opera house. He conducted a double bill of Orff's *Carmina Burana* and Stravinsky's *Oedipus Rex* in 1959, and the following year Monteverdi's *Orfeo* and Dallapiccola's *The Prisoner* — an unusual choice of repertoire, especially the Monteverdi, even for Stokowski. Music from the seventeenth century was not often in his programs and he did not seem to have much affinity or respect for the difficulties of performing early music. For the *Orfeo* production, Stokowski used a combination of ancient and modern instruments rather than transcribe the work for full symphony orchestra. The performances were imaginative and well-received.

The opera was conducted vigorously by Stokowski who used August Wenzinger's scholarly edition of the score. . . . The orchestral playing and choral singing were the least satisfactory elements in the production. . . . Dallapiccola's *The Prisoner*, which was paired with *Orfeo*, made its point with devastating effect. Stokowski's orchestra seemed to negotiate the intricacies of Dallapiccola with greater ingenuity than the baroque periods of Monteverdi. (Richard RePass, *Opera*, December 1960, pp. 815-816)

In the 1960-61 season Stokowski graduated to the more prestigious Metropolitan Opera House in New York and conducted eight performances of Puccini's *Turandot*. Dimitri Mitropoulos was scheduled to conduct but had taken ill so Stokowski was called in, although he was not in the best of health himself. He had just had a bad accident necessitating his coming to rehearsals in a wheel chair and conducting the first performance on crutches. Stokowski was not personally pleased with the production. He objected to both lighting and sets. With his penchant for involving himself in every detail of projects he works on, Stokowski took it to be perfectly correct that, as the conductor of an opera, he make sure each aspect of the production relate to the music. Unfortunately, the Metropolitan Opera does not work that way and never has. When the production was revived the next season, Stokowski conducted only two performances then withdrew to spend his time elsewhere.

The fact of the matter is that Stokowski's conducting had been heavily criticized by the New York press. In response Stokowski wrote a letter to the New York Times in which he claimed that there had not been enough rehearsal:

We were forced to present *Turandot* with only one full rehearsal. Everybody tried his utmost under these difficult conditions but the performances did not attain the artistic level I insist on for myself, due solely to the lack of rehearsal time. As additional stage rehearsals were not possible, I felt obliged to decline to conduct further performances. (*New York Times*, December 17, 1961)

However, the General Manager of the Metropolitan, Rudolf Bing, had quite a different viewpoint on the whole affair. He pointed out that the *Turandot* production was a revival from the previous season, that most of those involved had recently toured with it and that there had been as much rehearsal time allotted as to any other production at the Met. He laid the entire blame for shortcomings in the performance at the feet of Stokowski himself:

I regret to say that the discrepancies between the orchestra and the chorus and the chorus and the solo singers about which the press justifiably complained were equally apparent in last season's *Turandot* performances which had more than sufficient rehearsal. The reason for these discrepancies was not lack of rehearsal time. (*New York Times*, December 31, 1961)

Turandot was an unhappy experience for Stokowski and reinforced his impression that the opera house was not for him. A comment he made regarding this time in his career pretty well covers the subject:

The conditions of performance are not ideal; there is not enough time, not enough financial backing, to prepare opera thoroughly ... when we did *Wozzeck* a long time ago, I had the very great fortune to do it with Robert Edmond Jones, an instinctive dramatist in every way. He designed the costumes, the decor; he did the lighting; he did everything. But such men are rare. Jones is not with us any longer. It is hard to find persons today who combine all the talents he had. When I conduct opera, I am sometimes disappointed. It is nobody's fault; it is conditions. When I conduct a concert, I have a first-class orchestra and enough rehearsals. I do not do the concert unless I have four rehearsals. We can usually make a performance that approximates an ideal, whereas with opera it is much more difficult. (*Opera News*, February 24, 1962)

Just prior to his resignation from the Houston Symphony and about the same time he was conducting at the New York City Opera, Stokowski returned to conduct the Philadelphia Orchestra. It had been 19 years since he last stood before this orchestra. He had left in 1941 amid bitterness on both sides and it had taken nearly two decades to heal the wounds. Stokowski's efforts to raise money for his grandiose schemes had caused the board of the Philadelphia Orchestra no end of difficulty. Certain board members had been only too glad to be rid of him. Following his resignation Stokowski had made it a point of principle never to go back to Philadelphia and it was said that when he travelled through the city, he pulled the curtains down on his train window. His successor, Eugene Ormandy, willing to do whatever the board thought necessary, had proven to be much more co-operative than Stokowski. He is an excellent musician and he has maintained the highest possible standard of playing in the orchestra, but he lacks Stokowski's interpretative flair and his concerts were dull in comparison. With Stokowski, there was always something new at the Academy of Music. With Ormandy, it was routine and business as usual.

When Stokowski was finally invited back to conduct the orchestra in the spring of 1960, his reception was unprecedented: the audience was ecstatic and the orchestra was no less pleased. About one-third of the orchestra was still comprised of "Stokowski men," appointed during his years in charge of the orchestra, and under Stokowski they played the way they had always played for him — with a special tonal beauty possessed by no other orchestra. The program consisted of Mozart's *Marriage of Figaro* Overture, Falla's *El Amor Brujo*, Respighi's *Pines of Rome* and Shostakovich's Fifth Symphony. A few days later Stokowski took the orchestra and the same program to New York and received a tumultuous reception. Howard Taubman's review of the concert also mentioned the maestro's inimitable showmanship:

> The decor was dressed up with the most resplendent podium seen outside of a Hollywood studio. This was a silver circular affair, with two semi-circular steps, like those leading into a swimming pool. . . . The lavish tone was manipulated with infinite variety. . . . It was a program that gave all the choirs and many of the first-desk men a chance to shine, and how they played for the former head man! . . . After each piece Mr. Stokowski thanked the players and several times he applauded them. They in turn applauded him. (H. Taubman, *New York Times*, February 17, 1960)

The recordings Stokowski and the Philadelphia Orchestra made together after their momentous reunion are reminders that great conductors need great orchestras. All Stokowski's years of wandering as a guest conductor working with inferior orchestras were a waste of his talents. With the Philadelphia Orchestra, Stokowski was, to the fullest extent possible, himself again. He could assume the ultimate in virtuosity and go on to concentrate on the smallest details of interpretation. After listening to Stokowski's lack-lustre recordings with the Houston Symphony, it comes as a pleasant surprise to hear Stokowski and the Philadelphia in the love music from *Tristan und Isolde* by Wagner which they recorded for Columbia.

Stokowski's return to his old orchestra was one of his greatest triumphs and it led to annual visits to Philadelphia as a guest conductor. But before long he had embarked on a project which demanded far more of his time and energies. At the age of 79 he decided to found yet another orchestra, the American Symphony, which according to Stokowski, was created to give gifted young players the chance to gain some orchestral experience. It was also formed, however, to give Stokowski his own orchestra in New York. Time and again in his career he

Stokowski conducting the American Symphony Orchestra in Carnegie Hall at a 1969 Sunday afternoon rehearsal of Rimsky-Korsakov's *Capriccio Espagnol*. Stokowski is wearing a morning coat, reserving his more formal attire for evening concerts.

Andrzej Panufnik and Stokowski in the Church of St. John the Divine, New York, during rehearsal for the 1970 première of Panufnik's *Universal Prayer*. (Photo: Hoeffler)

Stokowski in his late teens.

The toast of Philadelphia, Stokowski in his early fifties.

Stokowski with Matthias Bamert (Assistant Conductor of the American Symphony) and Ainslee Cox (Associate Conductor) in Philharmonic Hall, New York, 1971. (Photo: Hoeffler)

Members of the horn section of the American Symphony being directed by Stokowski in the finer points of Tschaikovsky's Fourth Symphony, 1971. (Photo: Hoeffler)

Stokowski conducting the American Symphony in Carnegie Hall in a 1971 rehearsal of Beethoven's *Eroica*. (Photo: Hoeffler)

Characteristically surrounded by children, Stokowski watches a baseball game in Central Park, New York, 1969. (Photo: Hoeffler)

Stokowski, trying out his pitching arm with members of the American Symphony. (Photo: Hoeffler)

Stokowski, age 91. (Photo: Hoeffler)

At work in his study overlooking New York's Central Park. (Photo: Hoeffler)

had returned to New York, often maintaining a residence there even when he was a permanent conductor
elsewhere. He had wanted very much to become the
conductor of the New York Philharmonic in the late
1940s. For a variety of reasons conditions were never
right for him to settle in this city with his own orchestra.
Finally, nearing 80 years of age, Stokowski took matters
into his own hands — he planned his new orchestra's
programming, booked the hall, arranged the financing
and began to audition the players. Unfortunately, it was
not to be as easy as that. By the summer the financial
support collapsed. The American Symphony had its
first crisis before it had even given a concert and its
future seemed extremely doubtful. Stokowski saved the
day by underwriting the cost of the orchestra's first
season from his own pocket. In each of the nine succeeding seasons he put more money in as needed and
conducted without fee.

The American Symphony gave its first concert on
November 15, 1962 in a program which included a
Gabrieli *Sonata for Brass*, Bach's Toccata and Fugue in D
minor, Beethoven's Piano Concerto No. 1 with soloist
Susan Starr, and the Symphony No. 6 by Shostakovich.
The reviews were generally favourable:

Leopold Stokowski created the first new orchestra to be heard
here in 25 years.... After some 10 hours of rehearsal, qualities of
sound associated with this conductor were apparent in dynamics
and in colour, the more remarkable in this case because the
players were unfamiliar and youthful. (Carl Sigmon, *Musical
America*, December, 1962)

There were five other concerts that season and the
orchestra was on its way. Once again, Stokowski had put
together a first-class orchestra of talented and enthusiastic young players, many of them straight out of
school and without much professional experience.

Stokowski had always worked well with young people and rather enjoyed the opportunity to mould willing, young musical minds.

The orchestra's first recording was characteristic Stokowski repertoire in that it was a piece scarcely anyone else knew — the *Negro Folk* Symphony by William Dawson. The composer was born in Alabama in 1899, studied at the Tuskeegee Institute in his home state and went on to Kansas City and Chicago for further studies, returning to Tuskeegee as director of the Institute in 1930 The *Negro Folk* Symphony, begun in the 1920s and completed in 1932, was given its première by Stokowski and the Philadelphia Orchestra two years later. After the first performance of the work Dawson made several trips to Africa and his experiences there led him to revise the symphony. It is this later version that Stokowski and the American Symphony recorded in 1963 and it reflects African rhythms and feelings more directly than the former.

Nearly every Stokowski program with the American Symphony contained new music or a novelty of some sort, the most remarkable event being the long overdue first performance of Charles Ives' Symphony No. 4 which the orchestra premièred in its third season (1964-65). Completed in 1916, it took half a century and the 82-year old Leopold Stokowski to bring the work before the public and it turned out to be a block-buster. One of Ives' longest and most complex pieces, it is also a near masterpiece. The style of the music is typical Ives, with quotations from dozens of American popular songs, hymns and marches but on a scale larger than anything he had composed before. At one point in the score so much is happening in so many different rhythms that three conductors are required to keep it all going. A wordless chorus is added to the general tumult at the end of the fourth movement.. The most impressive and stunning movement is the second, a kind of *scherzo* with quotations from "Turkey in the Straw," "Yankee Doodle," "Camptown Races" and many more, creating an effect of distinctively American music based on indigenous sources, yet without the safe and soothing harmonies of an Aaron Copland. This is music of disturbing intensity. It is also a conductor's nightmare. That Stokowski was able to pull it off in his 80s is little short of incredible. Even with six extra rehearsals funded by the Rockefeller Foundation, it was no mean feat. Because Stokowski was the first to conduct this horrendously complex music, other conductors have felt they too had to rise to the challenge. The beneficiary of all this conductorial competitiveness has been the music of Charles Ives.

During his years with the American Symphony Stokowski held auditions every afternoon for two hours putting the best players on a waiting list for the orchestra. Stokowski took this auditioning process very seriously and obviously enjoyed being able to hear and make use of so much talent. Unlike most orchestras the American Symphony had a large turnover, not because so many players were fired, but because they were in such demand elsewhere and a position in the American Symphony was not, in itself, a full-time job. In fact, it was very much a free-lance job, something Stokowski seemed to prefer. Players were hired for one concert at a time rather than for the entire season, meaning that Stokowski was free to replace a musician if he so wished without breaking a contract or a commitment.

With the American Symphony Stokowski assumed a role he was very fond of — that of teacher. In rehearsals he was often severe and authoritarian, hoping to encourage his young players to do their best, and they did. He also devised a motto for the orchestra which he stated as follows:

Every rehearsal must be better than the last. Every concert must be better than the last. We must never be satisfied because upwards in quality is without limit. What can be done is limitless, particularly with the modern orchestra because the modern orchestra is extremely complex. To have a good relation between individual players and other individual players, or groups with other groups; to have that which we call *ensemble* — that is difficult. That is why we are trying, every concert and every rehearsal to do better than the last. (*Music Journal*, May 1968, p. 38)

One of the most unusual and provocative recordings Stokowski made with the American Symphony was the Beethoven *Emperor* Piano Concerto with Glenn Gould as soloist. The two musicians had never worked together before and they barely knew each other, but they both had a reputation for taking a fresh and often unexpected approach to the music they performed. The collaboration was bound to be something out of the ordinary. When they met to discuss their performance Gould suggested that it should either be very fast or very slow. Stokowski opted for the latter approach, resulting in a performance which, in Gould's words, is "very slow, very grandiose and Napoleonic with lots of tassels on the shoulder." Both Gould and Stokowski tire of doing standard pieces in the same way each time and they love to experiment. In Stokowski, Gould found an ideal partner who could adapt to his whims with no trouble at all:

That was a very happy experience. It was also very funny, because at the first rehearsal with the American Symphony, Stokowski, in his most elegiac frame of mind mounted the podium — and you know these are mostly young players who haven't had a great deal of experience with the standard concerto repertoire as yet — and he said, "Ladies and gentlemen, remember the *Eroica*." That's exactly what we did. We did a sort of *Eroica* Symphony with piano *obbligato*. (*Glenn Gould: Concert Dropout*, Columbia recording BS15)

While Gould's and Stokowski's intentions are understandable, the recording is not all that successful. It might have been a good idea for them to have played the work together in public a few times, as insufficient preparation seems to have gone into the performance. It is different, especially on Gould's part, almost to the point of being perverse, with odd tempos, odd phrasing, odd renderings of the trills, all for the sake of change. The effect, however, wears off very quickly. Nevertheless, one may be glad they had a go at the *Emperor*. More, not less interpretative freedom is required in music-making these days. The Goulds and the Stokowskis may be infuriating, but they are never boring, and they constantly challenge old prejudices and test the limits of the imagination.

For Gould and Stokowski this recording was the beginning of a series of projects initiated by Gould, including the preparation of a radio documentary on Stokowski as well as an interview for television. Both men are futurists who enjoy speculating about what is yet to come and feel not the least bit inhibited by their lack of specialist knowledge. These programs, full of oracular pontification, reveal a great deal about the personalities of the two men, and rather less concerning the nature of the world. Discussing almost any subject, Stokowski sounds not unlike a Zen Buddhist giving ever more cryptic answers to the point of absurdity. The listener is never sure whether he is listening to a man of great wisdom or an inspired bluffer.

Stokowski and the American Symphony certainly enlivened concert-going in New York during the 1960s. By the nature of its programming, the orchestra helped to develop a new, mostly young audience comprised of people turned off by the older and better established orchestras with their conservative repertoire, well-heeled committees and super-formal atmosphere. But Stokowski was nearly 80 when he created the orchestra

Beethoven's Third Symphony and Rachmaninoff's Third Symphony. One interesting two-record set from RCA has two performances of Dvorak's *New World* Symphony: a 1927 version with the Philadelphia Orchestra and a 1973 version with the New Philharmonia Orchestra.

later re-mixed to bring out individual voices. While they are certainly exciting and vivid, many critics feel Phase Four discs give an unreal sound picture of what a symphony orchestra is really like, and a gross distortion of the composer's intentions. Phase Four engineers, however, reply that they are not aiming at concert hall realism but at a new sound experience and effects not possible in the concert hall. Recording, they believe, is a unique medium and ought to be exploited as such. They also point out that often this recording technique enables the listener to hear things that are inaudible or which might pass unnoticed in a concert performance.

The Phase Four recordings seem to be aimed at a mass audience, perhaps hi-fi lovers rather than music lovers, and for this reason, most of the releases in this series include very familiar repertoire. Stokowski has recorded many such pieces for Phase Four but he has also managed to slip in something well off the beaten track — an album consisting of the Second Orchestral Set by Charles Ives and *L'Ascension* by Oliver Messiaen. Connoisseurs may feel that Phase Four recordings distort rather than enhance music, but Stokowski's involvement with this new process is consistent with his interest in the very latest recording techniques, and also reflects his life-long desire to bring symphonic music to a wider audience. In 1972, when Stokowski and the London Symphony celebrated the 60th anniversary of their first concert together by performing the identical 1912 program consisting of works by Wagner, Brahms, Glazunov and Tchaikovsky, a recording of the actual concert was issued as a two-record set by Decca-London.

Stokowski now lives in England. He does not travel much and gives no public concerts, but he continues to make recordings, most recently for RCA and Desmar. It is remarkable that in his nineties Stokowski is recording many works for the first time ever, including and could not be expected to carry on for ever. In 1972, at the age of 90, he decided he had carried the artistic, administrative and financial responsibility for the American Symphony long enough. He was past coping with life in New York City as well. He left for England and almost complete retirement. Shortly afterwards, he stopped giving public concerts, although he has continued to make recordings. Some years before he had decided that a conductor can achieve much better results on a recording anyway:

> In recording nothing is ever done less than twice, and this is why a recording done by an honest person is always better than a concert performance. (Interview with Robert Charles Marsh, *High Fidelity*, April 1961)

Stokowski first conducted the London Symphony 60 years before in 1912, but after his appointment to the Philadelphia Orchestra that same year, he did not often get a chance to appear in England. A notable exception was his visit on the occasion of the Festival of Britain in 1951 during which time the recording of Rimsky-Korsakov's *Scheherazade*, discussed earlier, was made. Regular Stokowski visits and recordings began only in 1959. In that year he recorded a Debussy-Ravel album with the London Symphony, returning almost annually after that. He led a memorable performance of Schoenberg's *Gurrelieder* at the Edinburgh Festival in 1961 and an equally fine Mahler Second Symphony at the Royal Albert Hall in 1963. In 1964 he signed a contract with Decca Records to make albums in their new Phase Four series. Phase Four is a system of recording which, up until that time, had been used only for pop music. It was thought to be unsuitable for classical music because of its somewhat gimmicky sound. The system makes use of an elaborate multi-miking technique, recording on separate channels of sound which are

6
Stokowski the Interpreter:
Music Before 1800

Stokowski has shown almost no interest at all in music composed before 1800, conducting very little Mozart or Haydn in his career and very few performances of music by Bach or Handel in their original versions. One can recall his performances of Monteverdi's *Orfeo* at the New York City Opera or occasional performances of the *St. Matthew Passion*, but such music has rarely been played by Stokowski, and in his long recording career he has never done a complete symphony by Mozart and only one by Haydn.

As a conductor Stokowski is associated with the great romantic composers of the nineteenth and twentieth centuries, from Tchaikovsky and Wagner through Rachmaninoff. Such music, with its wide dynamic, emotional and timbral range, brings out the best in him. With an eighteenth century orchestra, however, Stokowski cannot *do* much of anything and remain faithful to the style of the music. Historically, the conductor in the modern sense of the word did not even exist in the time of Handel, Bach, Mozart or Haydn. Performances were directed as necessary by the concertmaster or by the harpsichord *continuo* player. Interpretation, as we know it today, was not required or even thought desirable, and questions of tempo and balance were settled by the players themselves, often in consultation with the composer.

With this in mind, perhaps the modern conductor, needed neither for matters of interpretation nor for keeping the orchestra together, is well-advised to leave music from before 1800 alone. Unless he is prepared to lead performances of Bach or Mozart from the harpsichord or the concertmaster's chair and respect the discipline of eighteenth century style, he should spend his time on other repertoire. Moreover, relatively few conductors even know what style of playing is appropriate in Bach or Mozart. There are many reasons why Stokowski has ignored the music before 1800, but the most important is that the music does not need him.

On the other hand, it is also true that Stokowski is notorious for his arrangements of early music, particularly for his transcriptions of music by Bach. Stokowski's critics contend that it is misleading to say he has ignored the music of the eighteenth century and left it to others. Rather, he has systematically distorted it beyond all recognition. The music of Bach as played by Stokowski has nothing whatever to do with the original scores as Bach conceived them.

At this point, a distinction should be made between original orchestral works by Bach, Handel, etc. and transcriptions for orchestra of pieces originally composed for organ solo, solo violin, etc. Stokowski and others under his supervision made many transcriptions of Bach's music during the 1920s and 1930s on the grounds that, otherwise, the public might never hear his magnificent works, and it is a fact that the audience for concerts or recordings by the Philadelphia Orchestra was much greater than the audience for organ or violin recitals. When asked to defend his transcriptions Stokowski usually makes the following response:

> The important thing is not the instrument but the feeling expressed. You may not agree. Everyone has a right to his own opinion and so do I.

Stokowski also likes to point out that Bach himself was one of the world's great transcribers, taking music by Vivaldi and other lesser composers and arranging it for different instruments. What he fails to mention is that Bach and Vivaldi were contemporaries. The transcriptions do not present any problems of style. Stokowski, however, has transcribed Bach in a style completely alien to the original. The modern orchestra is different from anything imagined by Bach, and Stokowski asks it to play in a style that is suitable for Wagner or Tchaikovsky but not for Bach. "Feeling" may be more important than "instruments" but without the right instruments playing in the right style, perhaps it is not possible to arrive at that feeling.

Stokowski's reference to "feeling" is a variant of a claim he frequently makes that it is important to know the composer's intentions and he often alters a score on the basis that his changes more closely represent the composer's desires. If pressed, Stokowski will argue further that musical notation is primitive. A composer may do his best, but the marks on paper are not the music. It is the responsibility of the performer to see past these marks to the music. Even so, it is questionable whether what Stokowski sees when he goes beyond the notation is the same as what Bach saw when he wrote it down. The best evidence of a composer's intentions is, after all, these marks on paper. It would be safer for Stokowski to contend that his transcriptions of Bach are modern versions of the music. One does not have to accept these works as authentic Bach, or even as reasonably faithful to Bach, to enjoy them. They are acceptable as Bach imagined and expressed by Stokowski, a great virtuoso conductor of our time. Those listeners who know and love the originals will find it more difficult to enjoy Stokowski's renditions, but then Stokowski had another audience in mind. Some broad-minded listeners may feel that while a work such as the Passacaglia and Fugue in C minor comes off magnificently on the organ, it is also mightily impressive in Stokowski's orchestration. Perhaps it is a distorted look at Bach but it is still beautiful music and is admirably suited to the resources of the modern symphony orchestra.

While nearly all Stokowski's recordings of Bach have been of his own transcriptions, on several occasions he has done the music in more or less its original form. With the Philadelphia Orchestra in 1929 he recorded Bach's *Brandenburg* Concerto No. 2, a work scored for a small ensemble of solo strings with a few winds, most prominently a high trumpet. Stokowski's first mistake is to use too many strings resulting in a heavy, unwieldy sound that totally obscures the contrapuntal texture of the score. To make matters worse, he takes the slowest tempos imaginable, he alters dynamics, adds huge *ritardandi* and omits the harpsichord *continuo* part. In the slow movement Stokowski adds a full string section where none is indicated in the score and it plays running sixteenths which, again, are not in the score. Finally, in the last movement he takes the trumpet part down an octave in some places, completely ruining the characteristic sound of the music. Without much difficulty, in spite of the high trumpet, the Second *Brandenburg* Concerto is often performed today as originally scored. For no apparent reason Stokowski has destroyed both the letter of the score and the feeling of the music, obscuring nearly every virtue of the original and substituting nothing of value. However, it must be pointed out that Stokowski made this recording in 1929 and apparently, has never again played the work in this form let alone recorded it.

Stokowski is famous (or notorious) for his Bach transcriptions but he has applied himself to the music of other baroque composers as well. Over the years he has shown a special interest in Vivaldi's Concerto *Grosso* Op. 3 No. 11 in D minor, recording it three times — twice using his own transcription in 1934 and 1952 and once in the 1960s using something very close to the original. The dating of these recordings might suggest that Stokowski gradually came to see the error of his ways, realizing by the 1960s that no transcription was necessary. The inherent qualities of the music are obliterated in the earlier versions. There is no justification and no sense to the sudden swellings of brass choirs in music conceived for string orchestra and with dynamic markings appropriate to the period. Many concertos by Vivaldi are repetitious and uninteresting, but the consistently interesting and varied D minor concerto needs no embellishment from Stokowski to make it tolerable. It must be remembered, however, that when Stokowski first recorded the work the baroque string orchestra repertoire was all but unknown. As in the case of his transcriptions of the organ works of Bach, this music would have been played hardly at all if Stokowski had not arranged it for symphony orchestra. Today, Stokowski's transcription of Vivaldi's Op. 3 No. 11, like that of Bach's Second *Brandenburg* Concerto, is only an historical curiosity. In both cases, the originals are well-known and widely performed.

In recent years Stokowski has also performed and recorded Vivaldi's most famous work, *The Four Seasons*, a set of four violin concertos. As confirmation of the view that Stokowski has gradually altered his ideas about early music, his recording of *The Four Seasons* is based on the original version of the score, although he has not resisted the temptation to do a little souping-up. He uses far too many strings and employs an aggressive attack altogether foreign to the nature of the music.

If Stokowski has done less than justice to baroque music, he has been equally ill at ease with the music of the classical period which came immediately after — the music of Mozart and Haydn. Stokowski has conducted no Mozart operas and few of his concertos or symphonies. He has made just one recording of Mozart's symphonic music. This is the minuet movement from the Symphony No. 40 in G minor recorded with the Philadelphia Orchestra in 1919. The only complete Mozart works Stokowski has recorded commercially are the Serenade for Thirteen Winds K. 361 with the American Symphony, and the *Sinfonia Concertante* for four wind soloists and orchestra with the Philadelphia Orchestra.

Perhaps the most important composer ignored by Stokowski is Haydn. Stokowski has recorded only one of his works complete — the Symphony No. 53, the *Imperial*, with "his Symphony Orchestra" in 1949. The recording is quite good with virtually no audible alterations in the score indicating that Stokowski can conduct this music perfectly well if he wants to. But perhaps Stokowski does not find sufficient challenge for his qualities as a virtuoso conductor in the music of Haydn or any other composer before 1800. Most at home when he can exploit a vast dynamic range and explore the myriad colours of the symphony orchestra, he needs music for large orchestra composed in a style requiring conductorial supervision and intervention. This means that Stokowski's repertoire extends from the late romantics of the nineteenth century through the impressionist and neo-romantic composers of the twentieth century. He is at a loss in music which is based on contrapuntal texture (Bach), or structure and line (Mozart and Beethoven). For many years, therefore, he could not resist the temptation to alter these compositions to make them "more interesting" from his point of view; a sure indication that Stokowski did not really understand the music.

7
Stokowski the Interpreter: Beethoven

While the music of Beethoven (1770-1827) is, in some respects, quite different from that of Mozart or Haydn, to a conductor like Stokowski it still presents some of the same problems of eighteenth century music discussed in the last chapter. In our time the stature of conductors tends to be measured by performances of the Beethoven symphonies. Almost every major conductor of the recent past — Toscanini, Weingartner, Furtwängler, Reiner, Szell, Walter, Karajan and Bernstein — has done a fine recording of all nine. Stokowski is an exception. He has played them much less often and has yet to record the First, Second, Fourth or Eighth. Until a few years ago there was no recording of one of the greatest of them all, the *Eroica*. Stokowski has not demonstrated much interest in Beethoven even though there is a power and energy in his music far beyond anything contained in the classical compositions of the previous generation — a power to which, it would seem, Stokowski could respond. On the other hand, Beethoven's orchestra is still a smallish one of 40 or 50 players. He seldom wrote parts for trombones (Fifth,

Sixth and Ninth Symphonies only) and hardly ever asked for more than one percussion player (Ninth Symphony only).

The first Stokowski Beethoven symphony recording was an acoustical version of the Minuet movement from the Eighth Symphony, recorded in 1920 with the Philadelphia Orchestra. The playing seems fine and Stokowski takes no liberties with the score, but this is lightweight Beethoven requiring no particular insight to bring it off. Stokowski's first complete Beethoven symphony recording was the Seventh made in 1927 with the Philadelphia Orchestra. After that came the Fifth in 1931 and the Ninth in 1934 with the last movement done in English rather than the original German. In the next 10 years he recorded the Sixth for *Fantasia* and the Fifth a second time with the All-American Youth Orchestra in 1940. This was the full extent of Stokowski's Beethoven symphony recordings until 1945 — a grand total of three in about 30 years of recording.

In all, Stokowski has recorded the Fifth Symphony three times, the last being in 1969 with the London Symphony. In any conductor's performance of the Fifth, the first question that should be asked is: how does he treat the familiar four-note theme? (See example on following page.)

Are the opening bars an introduction to be played with emphasis or gravity, or are they to be thought of as a part of what follows and played in tempo? How long are the opening *fermatas* to be? How long are the pauses? There are vast differences among conductors on such matters. Toscanini tears into the music with great forcefulness, setting a rather quick tempo from the opening bars to which he adheres all the way through the movement. Karajan's approach is very similar. Both conductors play the opening bars not as introductory, but as part of the whole movement, and so take the same

93

tempo for both with no exaggerated holds or pauses.
Furtwängler sees the music differently. His opening
bars are far slower and dramatically supercharged in
contrast to his main tempo for the movement which is

94

much quicker. Klemperer is also a slow beginner, but he differs from Furtwängler in adopting the same slow tempo for the rest of the movement and in avoiding any hint of subjectivism. Of all these conductors, Stokowski is perhaps closest to Furtwängler in his general conception. He plays the opening bars very slowly with great emphasis and then speeds up. Unlike Furtwängler, however, Stokowski maintains greater objectivity and discipline. This description of Stokowski's Beethoven Fifth applies to his first two recordings of the work but not to his most recent. In his 1969 recording the opening bars are played much faster and at virtually the same tempo as the rest of the movement. By this time, it seems, Stokowski had become much less idiosyncratic and not so concerned with adding dramatic touches to the score to make it different.

The rarest Stokowski recording of the Beethoven Fifth is the one from 1931 with the Philadelphia Orchestra. Although it is not the best of the three recordings, and in spite of the fact that the sound is rather poor, it was one of the first LPs ever made and it was issued at a time when most records were 78s. The experiment was not a success. Most people did not then own two-speed players and the records did not last very long when played with the heavy pick-ups in general use. By 1940 only nine LPs remained in the catalogue and before long they were all withdrawn.

The abbreviated version of Beethoven's Symphony No. 6 in F major which Stokowski conducted for the film *Fantasia* has been a first experience with Beethoven for many people. In the context of the film, it has no doubt, been a pleasurable one. Stokowski recorded the complete Sixth with the New York City Symphony in 1945, and most recently with the NBC Symphony in 1954. This last also contains a short talk by Stokowski on the Sounds of Nature, reminiscent of the talks which accompanied his recordings in the late 1920s. Stokowski, however, is no Leonard Bernstein His talks have an Olympian aura about them. He comes across as stiff and somewhat pompous and his comments are superficial rather than penetrating or perceptive.

Stokowski's 1954 recording of the *Pastoral*, beautifully played with particular attention paid to orchestral colour, is much like the other two recordings he made of the work. But the slow movement is *so* slow, it seems to go on forever. This tempo is a serious drawback in Stokowski's conception of the work, although he certainly brings out much of the colour and lyricism in the music as few other conductors have done.

Stokowski has made three recordings to date of Beethoven's Symphony No. 7 in A major. The first, and in many respects the finest, is the 1927 recording with the Philadelphia Orchestra. The second dates from 1958 or 1959 with the Symphony of the Air, and the most recent was done in 1973 with the New Philharmonia. In 1927 Toscanini and Weingartner were the great Beethoven conductors of the day, but on the basis of his recording of the Seventh Symphony, it could be argued that Stokowski was in the same class. His Seventh is just as fast and just as well played as Toscanini's legendary version with the New York Philharmonic. Completely absent are the mannerisms which too often spoil Stokowski's other Beethoven recordings, and while the sound leaves a lot to be desired, one can still hear a great orchestra making music and a great conductor genuinely inspired.

The Beethoven Symphony No. 9 in D minor, as meaningful and as profound as anything the composer ever wrote, is generally regarded as a work of epic proportions. The first movement seems to move inexorably forward, culminating in a heaven-storming and shattering climax. The *scherzo* is Beethoven's largest movement in this form, and its timpani solo is a distinguishing feature. The third movement, based on two themes and two sets of alternating variations on these themes, is one of Beethoven's sublime creations, a seemingly endless flow of beautiful melody broken only near the end by trumpet fanfares. In the finale a dissonant outburst from the whole orchestra introduces a cello and bass recitative, the recollection of themes from earlier movements and finally voices — voices in a symphony for the first time ever — singing verses from Schiller's Ode to Joy in praise of universal love.

The Ninth Symphony is Beethoven's most grandly conceived work in any form save perhaps for the *Missa Solemnis* and *Fidelio*, and it seems to encompass more moods and feelings than most other pieces by any composer. From this brief outline of the work it will be apparent that its performance is a severe test for a conductor. Stokowski recorded the work for the first time in the 1930s with the Philadelphia Orchestra using an English translation for Schiller's verses in the last movement. He did not record it again until 1967 and on that occasion he reverted to the original German. There are places in the score of the Ninth Symphony where Beethoven has miscalculated, being, after all, deaf when he wrote it. Every conductor is well aware that some of the wind writing is completely covered by the strings if played as written. One common solution is to double the wind parts, using two rather than one player to a part. But in the recording studio, where balances can be adjusted on tape by bringing up one microphone and turning down another, this is not necessary. Stokowski's recording of the Ninth makes use of the studio's resources in this way, occasionally to good advantage, but more often to excess. Instead of the craggy blend of orchestral colours characteristic of Beethoven, distinct layers of sound are heard. The parts Beethoven wrote are clearer than ever before, yet they are detached from the rest of the orchestra. This kind of artificial balancing is annoying in the first movement and all but destroys the finale where basses and cellos in their recitative are boosted to the point where, loud but distorted, they lose all their characteristic tonal quality.

These engineering and production alterations, all presumably done with Stokowski's approval, are, as might be expected, in addition to changes Stokowski has made in the score itself. There is a passage at letter C in the *scherzo* scored for winds in the melody with strings hammering out the characteristic rhythm of the movement:

Often it is extremely difficult to hear what the winds are playing over the force of the strings. Stokowski, like many other conductors, solves this problem by adding french horns to the winds; not a bad solution if the horns are kept in decent perspective (as they are not by Mengelberg in his recording where they seem to have wandered in out of *Der Rosenkavalier*!). There are many other places, however, where Stokowski's changes are unique. In the last movement particularly, there are numerous *crescendos* and *diminuendos* added to the score which sound mannered and unconvincing. Most amazing of all is what Stokowski has done to the final bars. In the original, the *coda* ends with an ascending passage in the winds which is always drowned out by the accompanying triumphant noise from the brass and percussion. Stokowski, apparently feeling that Beethoven miscalculated here, has trumpets double the winds.

99

This is a touch of orchestration completely at odds with Beethoven's music. Trumpets as they existed in Beethoven's time could not play such a chromatic passage. Being a gifted composer, well aware of the limitations of the instruments at his disposal, Beethoven composed and orchestrated within these limitations, which, in fact, are an organic part of the Beethoven style and the Beethoven "sound." To suddenly introduce such an effect in the last bars of the Ninth is not only anachronistic, but stylishly incorrect and it cheapens and vulgarizes everything that has come before. That Stokowski could perpetrate such a thing shows that his understanding of Beethoven is questionable, and that he prefers superficial brilliance to the integrity of the music he is conducting.

On a more general level, these same criticisms may be applied to Stokowski's recording of the Beethoven Ninth as a whole. There is a certain power in the first movement but never any sense of repose and the slow movement is boring because Stokowski never allows the music to be naturally expressive. Everything is played with objectivity and without sufficient regard for variation in dynamics. To make matters worse, the performance is all on one disc and the side break is in the middle of a phrase in the slow movement! This is something that has been unthinkable since the days of 78s.

This recording of the Ninth represents Stokowski at very nearly his worst. It is a doctored version of both the score and of what the musicians played in the studio, that does credit to nobody. Stokowski has done a great deal over the years to develop the art of orchestral playing, and among his conducting colleagues he has always been noted for his interest in new technology in radio, films and recording. But when he became involved with Decca's Phase Four gimmickry, he really went too far. Technology can be used to bring music to an audience of millions who might otherwise never be able to hear it, yet it is questionable whether Phase Four brings people *music* at all. Beethoven's Ninth Symphony in Phase Four is like a different piece, and it is no improvement.

Stokowski recorded Beethoven's *Eroica* Symphony for the first time in 1975 at the age of 92. This work demands tremendous energy and concentration from a conductor and so it is not surprising that the performance should be inconsistent and wanting in finesse. Above all, it lacks Stokowski's usually uncanny control of orchestral sonority. The recording quality is poor with almost inaudible timpani and little dynamic range. But at least it is free from the studio manipulations of Stokowski's Phase Four recordings for Decca-London. By 1975 Stokowski was back with RCA, the company with which he began his recording career back in 1917. This is not a distinguished performance of the *Eroica* and perhaps Stokowski is not the man ever to do one. His talents seem to lie elsewhere.

8
Stokowski the Interpreter: Brahms

The four symphonies of Brahms present a challenge to a conductor almost equal to that of the Beethoven symphonies. On records Stokowski has demonstrated much more interest in Brahms than in Beethoven, recording the First Symphony four times, the Third Symphony twice and the Fourth Symphony three times. The First Symphony in particular has been a Stokowski signature tune. He conducted it at his first concert with the Philadelphia Orchestra in 1912, playing it often afterwards on other important occasions.

His first complete recording of a Brahms symphony in 1927 with the Philadelphia was also the First. It is one of the best recordings of the work ever made — a performance of indescribable beauty. Although it was produced in the early years of electrical recording, the extraordinary quality of the Philadelphia Orchestra under Stokowski comes through without any difficulty. The 1927 Otto Klemperer recording of this symphony with the Berlin State Opera Orchestra is pale and extremely dull in comparison. Even a 1937 recording of the work by Bruno Walter and the Vienna Philharmonic seems inferior. Stokowski's recording is infinitely richer in tone colour than either of these others.

In any Stokowski performance there are controversial elements, and his recording of the Brahms First Symphony has its share. In the first movement at bar 157, after the music has gradually subsided and become very quiet, things get going again in the violas. Brahms marked the viola part *piano* and most conductors play it as such. Stokowski, however, thinks it is more effective played *fortissimo*, an alteration which *is* very convincing. It makes this transition much more dramatic. Conductors have always differed in their approach to the final bars of the symphony. How fast should the *coda* go? Should the brass chorale be played more slowly or in tempo? Stokowski is among those conductors who believe in slowing up drastically the final chorale, but unlike anyone else, he interprets this passage in an extreme *legato* style. There is nothing in the score to justify this approach and it is, therefore, inappropriate. Nonetheless, this recording is a triumph for everyone concerned: the RCA engineers, the Philadelphia Orchestra and above all, Stokowski who created the orchestra and made it great. For some strange reason, this tremendous performance has never been re-issued on LP even though Stokowski has not recorded anything finer in his career.

Stokowski has made three recordings of the Brahms C minor Symphony but only one of the Second dating back to 1930. It would seem to be his least favourite Brahms Symphony, and perhaps this explains why the recording is such a boring, pedestrian effort. The Philadelphia Orchestra lacks the intensity of expression and beauty of tone which characterized its magnificent recording of the First Symphony just three years before. The quality of the recording, rather grey and lacking in bass, is partly to blame as well.

In 1929 Stokowski recorded Brahms' Third Symphony in F major and it too is not very successful. In this case, Stokowski's questionable ideas about the work hold some of the responsibility. He begins the first movement with a rather energetic tempo, slows to a crawl, shifts to a faster speed a few bars later, and then just as abruptly transfers back to the slower. This was no fleeting aberration. When Stokowski recorded this symphony with the Houston Symphony nearly 30 years later he made the same peculiar changes in tempo. Obviously Stokowski had a firm conviction of how the music should be played, but these tempo changes are illogical and unconvincing. While minor adjustments in tempo in a Brahms symphony are acceptable and even welcome, Stokowski's changes are too abrupt and too coldly calculated to be musically satisfying. It is probable that Furtwängler, had he done something similar, would have been totally convincing. The difference is that Furtwängler's interpretative quirks grew from within the music while Stokowski's seem imposed on it from without.

Other aspects of Stokowski's interpretation of Brahms' Third Symphony are also debatable, especially in the Houston recording. Stokowski took the second movement slowly in 1929, but in 1958 the music is scarcely moving at all. The third movement is played so fast that the characteristic turn in the horn melody becomes messy and graceless and the finale is far too slow to generate much momentum. Overall, there is an unwillingness to let the music breathe naturally as it must, in long lines. Rather than giving us the music of Brahms' Third Symphony, Stokowski offers a blueprint, and an eccentric one at that. More specifically, the 1958 Houston recording of the Third Symphony is a technical fiasco. The orchestra plays out of tune, instruments are spotlighted in the crudest imaginable way, the dynamic and tonal range is far more limited than it ought to have been in 1958, and there are even a couple of bad splices in which takes have been mismatched. It is inconceivable how Stokowski could have approved such a recording for release, but he did and so must accept responsibility for it.

Stokowski recorded the Fourth Symphony for the first time in 1933, again in 1940 and a third time in 1974. The best of them is, perhaps, the second with the All-American Youth Orchestra. The playing is remarkable enough to be mistaken for that of the Philadelphia Orchestra, and there are some wonderfully expressive moments in the slow movement. Unfortunately, the *scherzo* contains another example of arbitrariness of tempo. Stokowski begins very fast, then inexplicably slows to a crawl for the quieter second theme. In the last movement Stokowski all but ignores Brahms' *più allegro* marking near the end, thereby deflating the excitement of the *coda*. Strangely enough, at the end of the first movement Stokowski makes an enormous *accelerando* where none is indicated in the score and where none is needed. Throughout the performance Stokowski gives the impression of adding and subtracting from the score as he pleases with very little justification for what he is doing.

With the notable exception of Stokowski's 1927 recording of the First, his recordings of the Brahms symphonies are uneven, to say the least. In the previous chapter, the same conclusion was drawn concerning Stokowski's recordings of the Beethoven symphonies. These are the centrepieces of the symphonic repertoire — works which every conductor must play well to be considered a major interpreter. Stokowski is not at his best in Beethoven and Brahms; in fact, he does enough that is strange or questionable to cause one to doubt his judgement and understanding. That is not to say that Stokowski is not a great conductor after all. It is important, however, to define the limits of that greatness. Stokowski has more to contribute to an understanding and enjoyment of composers *other than* Bach, Mozart, Beethoven or Brahms. He remains a curiosity in the rather short history of conducting, however, in manifesting so little affinity for the music of these illustrious composers.

9
Stokowski the Interpreter:
Miscellaneous Composers

While Stokowski has been an unreliable interpreter of
Mozart, Beethoven and Brahms, there is a great deal of
music that he has conducted with consummate skill and
understanding. Wagner, for example, is one of the
composers for whom Stokowski has always had a special
flair and his recordings prove this point. Unfortunately,
Stokowski never recorded a complete Wagner opera or
music drama and he rarely conducted any of them in
public. His only experiences of Wagner in an opera
house were *Parsifal* and *Lohengrin* in Philadelphia more
than 40 years ago. Yet Stokowski has a superb grasp of
how the Wagner orchestra should sound, and how the
long Wagnerian melodic lines must be sustained and
allowed to unfold in their own time.

Just two years into his recording career which began
in 1917, Stokowski made his first Wagner recording —
the *Rienzi* Overture. This recording is of purely historical interest today. The poor quality of the sound does
not allow for an appreciation of either Wagner or
Stokowski. But Stokowski's 1947 recording of the same
work with the New York Philharmonic is another mat-

ter. It is virtually a master class on how to play the piece. This Overture is early Wagner and it is a side of the composer not generally admired. Stokowski makes one forget that the *Rienzi* Overture is often thought to be noisy and banal in the extreme. The writing for strings in the opening section has never been more eloquently realized and the brass interjections are beautifully judged for dramatic effect. Stokowski's very fast tempo for the *allegro* which follows makes the music thrilling instead of merely pompous. He slows up for the expressive cello theme at the end of this brassy *allegro* section to good effect, even though there is nothing in the score to indicate a change in tempo. In the *coda*, he really takes off, topping the excitement which has come before with even more dazzling playing. In this case, the liberties Stokowski takes in the score make sense and enhance the music.

Wagner's greatest achievement was the monumental *Ring* cycle of music dramas, yet Stokowski never recorded even a single complete Act from any one of them. The most extensive excerpts he recorded are contained in an RCA album made in Philadelphia in 1934. This is a typical Stokowski production. For the most part the original vocal parts are replaced by instruments in the orchestra, but there is a vocal portion tacked on as a finale. The whole excerpt is actually four selections from different places in *Die Walküre* — a bit from Act 2 Scene 4, the beginning of Act 3, a few bars from Act 3, Scene 3, and finally "Wotan's Farewell," the set piece for bass voice and orchestra which ends the work. There does not seem to be a musical or dramatic point to what Stokowski has pasted together, but he does bring to the concert platform some of the best music from *Die Walküre*. The soloist, Lawrence Tibbett, one of the great American opera stars of the day, was not particularly well-known for his Wagner roles but on the evidence of this recording perhaps he could have been. It is a fine effort by all concerned with accolades due most particularly to the strings of the Philadelphia Orchestra.

Stokowski has made quite a number of arrangements of bits and pieces from the Wagner music dramas. In addition to *Die Walküre* he has done comparable compilations from *Tristan, Das Rheingold, Siegfried, Die Götterdämerung* and *Parsifal*. He has also played the usual Wagner Preludes and orchestral bleeding chunks which the composer himself selected for concert performance.

The most memorable recordings by Stokowski of Wagner's music are generally those he made with the Philadelphia Orchestra in the 1930s. The sumptuous tone and variety of colour the Philadelphia was capable of producing were well suited to Stokowski's conception of Wagner. He has never achieved quite the same results with any other orchestra. Nevertheless, there are some performances worth mentioning. Stokowski's synthesis of music from *Parsifal* recorded with the Houston Symphony is not at all bad. While one misses the sound of the Philadelphia strings, at least, unlike the ancient Philadelphia recordings, a great deal of what is going on in the orchestra can be heard. It is much easier on the ears. *Parsifal*, a slow-moving, mostly quiet piece characterized by an almost endless flow of melody, is not exciting in the same way that *Tristan* or *Götterdämerung* are. It can neither be hurried nor made grander than it is. There are magnificent processionals in *Parsifal*, powerful enough to raise the roof, but Stokowski has not included them in his synthesis, choosing instead the often-played Good Friday Spell, a concert arrangement by Wagner himself from Act 3 Scene 1, and his own arrangement of excerpts from other parts of Act 3. Apart from the dubious coherence of the synthesis, as a whole it is a masterly performance conceived in such a way as to bring to the fore the latent impressionism in the music.

Some of Stokowski's recent Wagner recordings were made in London in 1966 using the notorious Phase Four technique. As has already been pointed out, Phase Four brings out the worst in Stokowski, emphasizing the vulgarity of his conducting while destroying his ear for orchestral balance and colour. Yet the members of the London Symphony play splendidly for Stokowski, most notably Barry Tuckwell in the horn solos in "Siegfried's Rhine Journey" from *Die Götterdämerung*. A peculiarity of this performance is that Stokowski does not begin and end the excerpt, as others do, in the places specified by Wagner in his concert version of this excerpt. Instead, Stokowski goes on past the usual ending, and then abruptly finishes where there really is no stopping point, so that the listener is left hanging — waiting for the next note.

Another composer for whom Stokowski has shown a great affinity is Sibelius. A champion of the Finnish composer's music all his life, Stokowski gave the first performances in the United States of the Fifth, Sixth and Seventh Symphonies, made the first recording of the Fourth Symphony and went to Finland to conduct and become acquainted with the composer. Stokowski has always been attracted to brilliant and colourful music, and he has a special gift for making an orchestra sing and sound enormously powerful. His performances of the Sibelius symphonies are evidence of this. Stokowski's special talents as a conductor seem to have drawn him more to the earlier symphonies with their greater full-blooded romanticism, as opposed to the thematically tighter and more austere later symphonies.

The Fourth Symphony is a transitional work, far less melodic, far less bombastic, and far less attractive on first hearing than any of the other symphonies of

Sibelius. Stokowski has not played the work very often but he did make the first recording of it in 1932 with the Philadelphia Orchestra in a performance which would have undoubtedly pleased the composer. The Philadelphia strings produce a magnificent sound and all the wind solos are handled with finesse and temperament. The only major criticism that might be made is that Stokowski greatly slows down for the final pages, although this is not indicated in the score. Sibelius specified the *ritardando* he wanted by lengthening the note values. Still, Stokowski's change does sound well and many conductors have done likewise.

In the 1950s Stokowski recorded the First and Second Symphonies of Sibelius and they too are excellent, with few alterations or eccentricities. Stokowski has also made a fine recording of the *Swan of Tuonela* with Mitch Miller as an impressive english horn soloist.

It is reasonable to assume, considering Stokowski's affinity for early Sibelius, that he might also be a fine interpreter of Tchaikovsky's music. But such is not the case. In his various recordings of Tchaikovsky symphonies, Stokowski is usually at his worst. This music needs an interpreter who will do more than obey the letter of the score. It is often highly personal in its expression and requires equal involvement and commitment on the part of the performer. This would seem to give a conductor plenty of opportunity to exercise interpretative freedom. Stokowski, however, abuses this license. In his recordings of the Fourth Symphony, for example, he not only bends the rhythm, he changes it. Not content to make the orchestration sound well, he must transform it altogether. Finally, his alterations in tempo destroy the structure of the music.

The trouble begins with the famous opening of the Fourth Symphony, a motto theme played by french horns and bassoons. After six bars the same fanfare is taken up by the trumpets. One of the outstanding features of this theme is the triplet:

In his 1927 and 1971 recordings Stokowski changes the triplet to a pair of sixteenths for reasons best known to himself. Stokowski compounds the sin in his 1971 recording by adding trumpets to horns and bassoons three bars before Tchaikovsky suggested they appear. In the earlier recording Stokowski also adds a vulgar slur to the phrasing, from the last note of bar four to the first note of bar five.

In the last movement of this symphony Stokowski has attempted another improvement on the composer. The *coda* section, beginning with a soft timpani roll and gradually increasing in volume and tension, is tremendously exciting. For the entire *coda* Tchaikovsky has indicated one tempo to which most conductors adhere, with excellent results. But not Stokowski. Every time the brass enter he pulls back the tempo and then shoots off

113

again. Particularly exaggerated in his 1971 recording, this interpretation makes complete nonsense of the music.

The 1953 recording of Tchaikovsky's Symphony No. 5 in E minor, brimming over with Stokowski's changes, some of which are quite radical, is even worse. To begin with, there are numerous cuts — four bars left out here, 16 there, and so on. While Tchaikovsky's music *is* repetitious to the point that for many listeners these cuts could easily pass unnoticed, they are difficult to condone. Further into the first movement *allegro* Stokowski makes some strange alterations in the transition to the bassoon theme at bar 321. The score calls for horns and strings gradually dying away and solo bassoon entering quietly in the same tempo. In the Stokowski version, *crescendos* have been added on the string chords, the horns are muted giving a totally different colour to the sound, and the first note of the bassoon solo is held much longer than the eighth note indicated in the score. In the third movement, at bar 56, Stokowski has tampered with another bassoon solo. As written, the bassoon and later the other winds play three eighth notes as pickup to the first beat of the next bar. Stokowski has changed the three eighths to one eighth, a dotted eighth and a sixteenth. Finally, at bar 550 in the last movement, Stokowski adds a slur — generally a simple addition, but in this case it changes the whole character of the music. The passage in question, the exciting final bars in the trumpets, is usually heard with each note separated or detached. Stokowski slurs the notes G sharp to A:

Molto meno mosso (♩.= 98)

*Slur added by Stokowski

115

Perhaps Stokowski's most appalling and inexplicable tampering with Tchaikovsky's music is to be found not in any of the symphonies, but in the tone poem *Romeo and Juliet*. The work ends with a long timpani roll *fortissimo* punctuated by sharp chords from the rest of the orchestra — a magnificent effect that never fails to excite and audience. (See example on following page).

Stokowski, for some reason, has eliminated the timpani roll and the *tutti* chords entirely, ending the work with quiet chords in the strings which do not even exist in Tchaikovsky's original.

In each of the examples cited where Stokowski has altered the score as Tchaikovsky wrote it, and as most of us know it, the first question is "why did he do it?" The music works perfectly well as it stands. Why change it? In none of these instances have musicologists or interpreters suggested weaknesses or embarrassments in the score. Stokowski's changes sound totally arbitrary, contrived and, in the case of the Tchaikovsky Fifth example, in bad taste.

10
A Summing Up

Conductors come and go. Many people regard them as little more than necessary evils, — ego-trippers who place themselves, literally, on pedestals higher than either the musicians they lead or the composers whose works they play. Beethoven's Fifth Symphony or Debussy's *La Mer* becomes simply a vehicle for conductor X, just as the Philadelphia Orchestra or the Berlin Philharmonic is a vehicle for conductor Y. Any orchestral player will relate what agony it is to put up with most conductors. Most composers tell the same story, and will further recount how they have to grovel and humble themselves to get a conductor to even look at their music let alone play it.

But orchestral players, composers and music-lovers all agree that there are exceptions. Some men are born to lead. As conductors, they possess an almost uncanny ability to make the best of what a composer has written, and to inspire even the most jaded orchestral players to give everything they have and more. They breathe life into music long thought boring or second-rate.

Stokowski is such a conductor. Although he has infuriated composers and musicologists by changing

118

scores at will, and tormented orchestral players with his authoritarianism, his aloofness and his egocentrism, he has also interested himself in more new music than any other conductor in the first half of the twentieth century. His première performances number in the several hundreds, and include most of the important works of the first half of the twentieth century. In the Philadelphia Orchestra he created one of the foremost ensembles of musicians the world has ever known. He has an obvious genius for selecting and training players. While many players may have disliked Stokowski personally, they would be the first to express pride in being a part of his orchestra. Over the years numerous listeners have been annoyed by his playing so much new or unfamiliar music, but in so doing, Stokowski has made concert-going unpredictable and exciting.

Perhaps Stokowski's most important characteristic is his insatiable curiosity. He has been a model of inquiring adventurism in a profession dominated by frustrated museum curators and paleontologists. In terms of repertoire, his record is matchless, but in other areas too he has been unique. His experiments with seating in the orchestra, with different types of instruments and with bowing, while not uniformly successful, reflect the keenness of his ear and his mind. He led the way in recordings in 1917 with early acousticals to the first electrical recording of a complete symphony in 1924. He made the first recording of sound on film in 1939, pioneered the broadcasting of concerts in the early 1930s and brought symphonic music into Hollywood films via Deanna Durbin and Walt Disney. The list of Stokowski innovations is practically endless.

An egomaniac Stokowski certainly has been, and much else besides. His greatest fault is his unreliability as an interpreter. Yet here too one can point to evidence of his untiring curiosity — his interpretations are often radically different from anyone else's because he never ceases to have new ideas about the pieces he conducts. For Stokowski admirers, it is simply a matter of indifference if critics find these ideas arbitrary, stylistically wrong, or tasteless.

The sound of the Philadelphia Orchestra was Stokowski's creation and thanks to recordings, it has been preserved for future generations. They will also be able to hear the Stokowski magic and individuality on a vast number of more recent recordings of music by Sibelius, Wagner, Tchaikovsky and Stokowski's transcriptions of Bach. In the eternal re-showings of the film *Fantasia* they will have the opportunity to see what a serious musician did with new technology and a popular medium. This is not a bad legacy for any artist, and when the history of twentieth century music is written and rewritten in years to come, Stokowski's name will be everywhere and inescapable. Who gave the American première of Mahler's Eighth Symphony, Berg's opera *Wozzeck*, Ives' Fourth Symphony, Sibelius' Seventh Symphony, Stravinsky's *Le Sacre du Printemps*, Strauss' *Alpine* Symphony, Shostakovich's Symphony No. 1, Rachmaninoff's Symphony No. 3? Which conductor made the first transcontinental tour of the United States with his orchestra? Who developed the concept of "free-bowing" in symphony orchestras? The answer to all these questions and countless more like them is the same: Leopold Stokowski.

Selected Bibliography

Aldrich, Richard. *Concert Life in New York 1902-1923*. New York: Putnam's, 1941.

Ewen, David. *Dictators of the Baton*. Chicago: Ziff-Davis Publishing, 1945.

Jacobson, Robert. *Reverberations: Interviews with the World's Leading Musicians*. New York: Morrow, 1974.

Kupferberg, Herbert. *Those Fabulous Philadelphians*. New York: Scribner's, 1969.

Mencken, H.L. *On Music*. New York: Knopf, 1961.

Reis, Claire R. *Composers, Conductors and Critics*. New York: Oxford University Press, 1955.

Roussel, Hubert. *The Houston Symphony Orchestra 1913-1971*. Austin and Houston: University of Texas Press, 1972.

Schanet, Howard. *Philharmonic: A History of New York's Orchestra*. Garden City, New York: Doubleday, 1975.

Stokowski, Leopold. *Music for All of Us*. New York: Simon and Schuster, 1943.

Stravinsky, Igor, and Craft, Robert. *Expositions and Developments*. London: Faber and Faber, 1962.

Szigeti, Joseph. *With Strings Attached*. New York: Knopf, 1947.

Taubman, Howard. *Music on My Beat*. New York: Simon and Schuster, 1943.

Wister, Frances Anne, *Twenty-Five Years of the Philadelphia Orchestra*. Philadelphia: Edward Stern and Co., 1925.

Discography

Stokowski's recording career falls into three parts. The Philadelphia era extended from October 22, 1917 to December 22, 1940. During the post-Philadelphia era he conducted other U.S. Orchestras, recording for RCA, Columbia, Capitol, Everest, United Artists and U.S. Decca. Since the early 60s Stokowski has also recorded outside the U.S. for English Decca/London, RCA, Unicorn MK, Pye, CBS, Desmar and Vanguard. Recording dates, where known, are given.

For his invaluble assistance in the preparation of this discography, I would like to thank Ivan Lund of Queensland, Australia.

Performing as soloists in these recordings are the following artists: **CELLO:** Emanuel Feuermann, Benar Heifetz, George Neikrug; **FLUTE:** Julius Baker; **HARP:** Edna Phillips; **HARPSICHORD:** Igor Kipnis, Wanda Landowska; **HORN:** David Gray; **ORGAN:** Nicholas Kynaston; **PERCUSSION:** Alfred Howard, Elayne Jones.

PIANO

Maro Ajemian	Alexander Kelberine
Olga Barabini	Kurt Leimer
Jeanne Behrend	Sylvan Levin
Henry Cowell	Jack Lowe
David del Tredici	Mary Binney Montgomery
Isabella di Carli	Serge Rachmaninoff
Glenn Gould	Raymond Viola
Percy Grainger	Arthur Wittmore
Dame Myra Hess	Gerson Yessin
William Kapell	

TRUMPET: Howard Snell; **VIOLIN:** Anahid Ajemian, Hugh Bean, Silvia Marcovici

SINGERS

Licia Albanese
Betty Lou Allen
Paul Althouse
Sheila Armstrong
Martina Arroyo
Virginia Babikian
Rose Bampton
Robert Betts
Kenneth Bowen
John Cameron
April Cantelo
Ruth Cathcart
Agnes Davis
Eileen Farrell
Brigitte Fassbaender
Warren Galjour
Guy Gardner
Clyde Hager
Heather Harper
Frederick Jagel
Martha Lipton
Eugene Lowenthal
Donald McIntyre
Robert Merrrill

Nan Merriman
John Mitchinson
Anna Moffo
Nicola Moscona
Doris Okerson
Carlotta Ordassy
Louise Parker
Jan Peerce
Margaret Price
Norma Proctor
Regina Resnik
Abrasha Robofsky
Nicola Rossi-Lemeni
Regina Sarfaty
Roger Stalman
Risë Stevens
Lawrence Tibbet
Helen Traubel
Shirley Verrett
Jeannette Vreeland
Helen Watts
Doris Yarick
Alexander Young

SPEAKERS

Jean-Pierre Aumont
Benjamin de Loache
Bob Keeshan
Goddard Lieberson

Madelaine Milhaud
Basil Rathbone
Martial Singher

CHOIRS (preceded, in some cases, by abbreviations used in these listings)

	American Concert Choir
BBCWC	BBC Women's Chorus
	Curtis Institute Chorus
	Fortnightly Club
	Gregg Smith Singers
	Ithica College Concert Choir
JAC	John Alldis Choir
	Louis Halsey Singers
LSOC	L.S.O. Chorus
	Mendelssohn Club
NLC	Norman Luboff Choir
	Princeton Glee Club
RSC	Robert Shaw Chorale
RWC	Roger Wagner Chorale

124

| SC | Schola Cantorum |
| | Welsh National Opera Chorale |

"EXTRA" CONDUCTORS
David Katz and José Serebrier (in Ives' Symphony #4)

ORCHESTRAS (preceded by abbreviations used in these listings)

ASO	All-American Symphony
	All-American Youth
BPO	Berlin Philharmonic
CSO	Chicago Symphony
CPO	Czech Philharmonic
FNRSO	French National Radio Symphony
HRPO	Hilversum Radio Philharmonic
HBSO	Hollywood Bowl Symphony
HSO	Houston Symphony
LPO	London Philharmonic
LSO	London Symphony
LAPO	Los Angeles Philharmonic
NATPO	National Philharmonic
NBCSO	N.B.C. Symphony
NPO	New Philharmonia
NSO	New Symphony Orchestra of London
NYCSO	New York City Symphony
PO	The Philadelphia
PhO	Philharmonia
PSONY	Philharmonic-Symphony Orchestra of New York
RCASO	RCA Symphony
RPO	Royal Philharmonic
SFSO	San Francisco Symphony
SSO	Stadium Symphony (PSONY)
SRO	Suisse Romande
SOA	Symphony of the Air
SO	"His" Symphony Orchestra
USSRO	USSR Radio Symphony

BANDS
Band of the Grenadier Guards

All known commercially released Stokowski recordings are listed in this discography. North American and British numbers are given. Performances are listed chronologically. Catalogue numbers shown are usually for the original issue, although in some cases the number for the most widely distributed coupling is shown. Because of re-packaging and re-coupling, numbers can change. Consult current catalogues for availability.

QUAD
Some Stereo/Quad discs have been issued by RCA in the CD format. Nixa discs are all QS while the latest Columbia disc (Bizet) is only

available as a compatible SQ. Consult current catalogues for status of quad discs.

TAPE

Although many RCAs were issued on reel-to-reel four track stereo tapes, these are now discontinued. Most Decca/London material is in cassette format and other companies will undoubtedly follow suit. Again, current catalogues are the best guide to availability.

KEY TO RECORD IDENTIFICATION

78 RPM DISCS

V	= Victor	V M	= multiple set
C	= Columbia	M M, M X	= multiple set
D, DA, DB, E	= HMV		

LONG PLAY DISCS

ARL, AVM, CAL,
CRL, LCT, LM, LSC =   RCA/US
VCM, VCS, VIC,
VICS

L ... (STD) = RCA/US LPs issued in the early 30s, 18 of which
                     were Stokowski's

ARL, AVM, CRL, SB, SRS, VIC	RCA/UK
CL, M, ML, MS, Y	CBS/US
CBS	CBS/UK
S, SP, SSAL	EMI/US
ALP, BLP, WRC, 33c, SXLP	EMI/UK
IC	EMI/Germany
SPC	London
PFS, SPA, SDD, OPFS	E. Decca
CRI	CRI
DL	Decca/US
DSM	Desmar
BVS	Disneyland/UK
WDX	Disneyland/US
SDBR	Everest (all recorded 1958/59)
SCFL	Fontana/UK
MK	MK (Russia)
6500	Philips
PCNH	Pye
RHS	Unicorn
UAS	United Artists/US
IPL, MJA, PARNASSUS, OPUS	US "re-issue" labels with no company affiliation
BGS, VSC, VSD	Vanguard/US

78s are shown in regular face type. Acoustic 78s have an (a) after the number. Mono LPs are shown in italics while stereo LPs are shown in bold italics.

ADAM, Adolphe
  Giselle: Ballet Excerpts
    SO   16/5/50   *LM 1083*

126

ALBÉNIZ, Isaac
Fête Dieu à Seville (orch. Stokowski)
PO	27/9/28	V 7158	D 1888
NATPO	1976	*CBS 73589*	

AMIROV, Fikret
Azerbaijan Mugam
HSO	circa 1958/59	*SDBR 3032*

BACH, J.S.
Brandenburg Concerto #2
PO	27,28,29,/9/28	V M59	D 1708/10

Brandenburg Concerto #5
PO	25/2/60	*Y 33228*	*CBS 30061*

Suite #2 for Flute and Strings
Baker
SO	12,14/9/50	*LM 1176*

BACH, J.S. (orch. Stokowski)
Chorale, Jesus Cristus Gottes Sohn (Easter Cantata)
PO	5/4/37	V M401	
SO	8/8/50	*LM 1176*	
CPO (live)	7,8/9/72	*SPC 21096*	*PFS 4278*

Sonata #6 in E for Violin: Preludio
ASO	20/7/41	C 11983

Jesu, Joy of Man's Desiring
SO	8/8/50	*LM 1176* .	DB 21570

Luboff Choir
NSO	pub. 1962	*LSC 2593*
SO (orch. Schickele)		*BGS 70696*

Arioso, Cantata #156: Sinfonia
ASO	11/7/41	C MX541	
NBCSO	27/11/41	V 18498	DB 6150
LSO	pub. 1976	*ARL 1 0880*	

Birthday Cantata: Sheep May Safely Graze
SO	8/8/50	*LM 1176*

Luboff Choir
New SO	pub. 1962	*LSC 2593*
SO		*BGS 70696*

Sleepers Awake
LSO	pub. 1975	*ARL 1 0880*

Chorale, Ein Feste burg ist unser Gott
PO	28/10/33	V 1692	DB 2453
ASO	1941	M X219	
SO	pub. 1959	*S 60235*	
LSO	pub. 1976	*ARL 1 0880*	

Chorale Prelude, Aus der Tiefe rufe Ich
PO	15/3/30	V 7553	DB 1789

Chorale Prelude, Christ lag in Todesbanden
PO	4/4/31	V 7437	DB 1952

Chorale Prelude, Ich ruf zu dir Herr Jesu Christ
PO	13/10/27	V 6786	D 1464
PO	27/11/39	V M963	
PO	25/2/60	*Y 33228*	*CBS 30061*

Chorale Prelude, Num komm der Heiden Heiland
PO	7/4/34	V M243	DB 2274
PO	25/2/60	*Y 33228*	*CBS 30061*

127

Chorale Prelude, Wir glauben all' an einen Gott

PO	1/5/29	V M59	D 1710	
SO	25/7/50	*LM 1176*		
PO	25/2/60	*Y 33228*	*CBS 30061*	
CPO (live)	7,8/9/72	*SPC 21096*	*PFS 4278*	

Komm, Süsser Tod

PO	28/10/33	V M243	DB 2274	
ASO	8/7/41	C 11773		
SO	25/7/50	*LM 1176*		
SO	pub. 1959	*S 60235*	MFP 2062	
LSO	pub. 1975	*ARL 1 0880*		

Mein Jesu, was fur seelinweb

PO	28/11/36	V M401	DB 3405	
ASO	1/5/41	C 19004		
SO	25/3/50	*LM 1133*		
SO	pub. 1958	*SIB 6094*		
CPO (live)	7,8/9/72	*SPC 21096*	*PFS 4278*	

Fugue in G Minor (Great)

PO	7/4/34	V 1728

Fugue in G Minor (Little)

PO	17/3/31	V 7437	DB 1952
ASO	14/11/40	C 11 992	
SO	25/7/50	*LM 1176*	DB 21570
SO	pub. 1959	*S 60235*	
LSO	pub. 1976	*ARL 1 0880*	

Christmas Oratorio: Shepherd's Music

PO	30/4, 1/5/29	V 7142	D 1741
SO	pub. 1959	*S 60235*	
SO		*BGS 70696*	

Passacaglia and Fugue in C Minor

PO	28/1, 1/5/29	V M59	D 1702/3	*VCM 7101*
		VIC 6060		
PO	16/11/36	V M401	DB 3252/3	
ASO	4,5/7/41	C X216		
SO	15/3/50	*LM 1133*	*BLP 1074*	
SO	pub. 1959	*S 60235*		
CPO (live)	7,8/9/72	*SPC 21096*	*PFS 4278*	

St. Matthew Passion: My Soul is Athirst

PO	28/11/36	V M401	DB 3405
	: Es ist Vollbracht		
PO	22/10/34	V 8764	DB 2762
PO	8/12/40	V M963	

Prelude and Fugue #3 in E Minor

PO	16/11/37	V M963

Violin Sonata #2 in B Minor: Sarabande

PO	16/11/36	V M401
SO	pub. 1959	*S 60235*

Sonata #3: Andante Sostenuto

ASO	11/7/41	M X541

Sonata #4: Chaconne

PO	30/11/34	V M243	DB 2451/3
SO	25/3/50	*LM 1133*	
LSO	pub. 1975	*ARL 1 0880*	

Sonata for Clavier and Violin #4: Siciliano

PO	28/10/33	V M243	DB 2275
SO	25/3/50	*LM 1133*	

Trio-Sonata #1 in E Flat for Pedal Clavier: 1st Mov't.

PO	27/11/39	V M963	DB 6260

128

English Suite #2: Bourée #2

PO	15/1/36		DA 1639
SO	24/3/50	*LM 1133*	*BLP 1074*
SO	pub. 1959	*SP 8489*	

English Suite #3: Sarabande

PO	7/4/34	V M243	DB 2275

Suite #3 in D Major: Air on the G String

PO	15/1/36	V M401	DA 1605
ASO	11/7/41	C X220	
SO	pub. 1959	*SP 8458*	*SXLP 30174*
LSO	pub. 1976	*ARL 1 0880*	

Toccata, Adagio and Fugue in C Major: Adagio

PO	28/10/33	V M243	DB 2335

Toccata and Fugue in D Minor

PO	6/4/27	V 6751	D 1428	VCM 7101
		VIC 6060		
PO	26/11/34	V 8697	DB 2572	
ASO	4/7/41	C X219		
PO (orch. Wood)	1940	*WDX 101*	*BVS 101*	
SO	22/3/47	*LM 2042*	*BLP 1074*	
SO	pub. 1958	*S 60235*	*SMFP 2145*	
CPO (live)	7,8/9/72	*SPC 21096*	*PFS 4278*	

Prelude and Fugue #2 in C Minor: Fugue

PO	7/4/34	V 1985	DB 2453

Prelude and Fugue #8 in E Flat Major: Prelude

PO	12/10/27	V 6786	D 1464
ASO	11/7/41	C X541	
CPO (live)	7,8/9/72	*SPC 21096*	*PFS 4278*

Prelude and Fugue #24 in B Minor: Prelude

PO	2/5/29	V 7316	D 1938
SO	15/3/50	*LM 2042*	

BARBER, Samuel

Adagio for Strings

SO	2/9/56	*SIB 6094*	*SXLP 30174*

BARTOK, Bela

Sonata for Two Pianos and Percussion
Yessin, Viola, Jones, Howard,

SO	27/3, 3/4/52	*LM 1727*	

Music for Strings, Percussion and Celeste

SO	pub. 1959	*SP 8507*	*WRC SCM 69*

Concerto for Orchestra

HSO		*SDBR 3039*

BEETHOVEN, Ludwig van

Ruins of Athens: Turkish March

NBCSO	9/2/55	*LM 2042*

Symphony #3

LSO	pub. 1975	*ARL 1 0600*

Symphony #5

PO	1931	*L 7001 (STD)*	
ASO	14/11/40	C M451	
LPO	9,10/9/69	*SPC 21042*	*PFS 4197*

Symphony #6:

PO (abridged)	1940	*WDX 101*	*BVS 101*
NYCSO	20/2/45	V M1032	*CAL 187*

: plus Sounds of Nature

129

```
            NBCSO          18/19/3/54     LM 1830      ALP 1268
       Symphony #7
            PO             6,15/4/27      V M17  D1639/43
                                          PARNASSUS 5
            SOA                           UAS 8003
            NPO            17,18/1/73     SPC 21139    PFS 4342
       Symphony #8: Allegretto
            PO             20/5/20        V 6243(a)    DB 385(a)
       Symphony #9
            Davis, Cathcart, Betts, Lowenthal, Chorus (in English)
            PO             30/4/34        V M236       DB 2327/35

            Harper, Watts, Young, McIntyre, LSOC
            LSO            20,21/9/67     SPC 21043    PFS 4183
       Piano Concerto #5
            Gould
            ASO            1,4/3/66       MS 6888      CBS 72483
       Egmont Overture
            NPO            17/1/73        SPC 21139    PFS 4342
       Leonora Overture #3
            NATPO          March/76       PCNHX 6
       Coriolanus Overture
            LSO            pub. 1975      ARL 1 0600


BEN-HAIM, Paul
    Suite, From Israel
            SOA            1958/59        UAS 8005


BERGER, Theodor
    Rodino Giocoso
            SO             pub. 1958      SP 8485


BERLIN, Irving
    God Bless America
            ASO            1940           C 17204


BERLIOZ, Louis Hector
    Damnation of Faust: Dance of the Sylphs
            SO             15/2/51        LM 9029
            LSO            22,23/6/70     SPC 21059
                         : Rakoczy March
            PO             12/10/27       V 6823   D 1807   VCM 7101
                                          VIC 6060
            NATPO          Nov./75        PCNH 4
    Symphonie Fantastique
            NPO            19,20/6/68     SPC 21031    PFS 4160
    Roman Carnival Overture
            NATPO          March/76       PCNHX 6


BIZET, Georges
    L'Arlésienne: Suite #1
            PO             3,4/5/29       V M62        D 1801/2
            SO             29/2/52        LM 1706
                         : Suite #2
            SO             5/3/52         LM 1706
            NATPO          23,25,27/8/76  M 34503      CBS 76589
                         : Spanish Dance
            PO             27/1/22        V 1113(a)
```

130

Carmen: Prelude to Act 1
PO	8/5/19	V 796(a)	
PO	10/5/27	V 1356	E 531

: Changing of the Guard, Smugglers March
PO	30/4/23	V 1017(a)	DA 612(a)

: Prelude to Act IV
PO	10/5/27	V 1356	E 531

: Incidental Music
PO	30/4, 2/5/27	V 6873/4	D 1618/1816	*L 1000 (STD)*
NYCSO	28/2/45	V M1002	DB 9505/8	*LM 1069*
NATPO	23,25,27/8/76	*M 34503*	*CBS 76589*	

Symphony in C
SO	20/3/52	*LM 1706*

BLOCH, Ernest
America — An Epic Rhapsody
America Concert Choir,
SOA	*VSD 2056*

Schelomo
Feuermann
PO	1939	V M698 DB 5816/8	*CAL 254*

Neikrug
SOA	1958/59	*UAS 8005*

BOCCHERINI, Luigi
String Quintet in E Major: Minuet (orch. Stokowski)
PO	27/1/22	V 798(a)	HMV 2-947(a)
PO	4/5/29	V 7256 D1864	*CAL 120*
SO	pub. 1958	*SP 8458*	*SXLP 30174*

BORODIN, Alexander
In the Steppes of Central Asia
SO	14/4/53	*LM 1816*

String Quartet in D: Nocturne (arr. Sargent)
SO	pub. 1958	*SP 8415*	*SXLP 30174*

Prince Igor: Polovtsian Dances
PO	29/4/25	V 6514

: Polovtsian Dances (orch. Stokowski)
PO	5/4/37	V M499 DB 3232/3	*CAL 203*
SO & Chorus	8/2/50	*LM 1054*	DA 2073

Welsh Nat Opera Chorale, JAC
RPO	16,17/6/69	*SPC 21041*	*PFS 4189*

BRAHMS, Johannes
Hungarian Dance #1 (orch. Stokowski)
PO	21/5/20	V 1113(a)	
PO	17/3/34	V 1675	DA 1398
		CAL 123	
HBSO	23/8/46	V 10-1302	
NATPO	Nov./75	*PCNH 4*	

Hungarian Dance #5
PO	22/10/17	V 797(a)

Hungarian Dance #6
PO	24/10/17	V 797(a)

Serenade #1
SOA	pub. 1961	*DL 710031*

: Minuet

PO	1934	V 1720	DA 1462

Symphony #1

PO	25,26,27/4/27	V M15	*LM 15 (STD)*
PO	1936	V M301	DB 2874/8
HBSO	1/8/45	*LM 1070*	
LSO (live)	14,15/6/72	*SPC 21090/1*	*OPFS 3/4*

Symphony #2

PO	29,30/4/29,		
	15/3/30	V M82	D 1877/82

Symphony #3

PO	25,26/9/28	V M42	D 1769/73 *CAL 164*
HSO		*SDBR 3030*	

         : **Poco Allegretto**

PO	18/4/21	V 6242(a)	

Symphony #4

PO	4/3/33	V M185	*LM 185 (STD)*
ASO	1940	C M452	
NPO	pub. 1975	*ARL 1 1317*	

BYRD, William
Pavan for the Earl of Salisbury (orch. Stokowski)

PO	19/4/37	V 1943	DA 1637

Pavan, Earl of Salisbury and Galliard

LSO	1975	*SPC 21130*	*PFS 4351*

The Fitzwilliam Virginal Book: Gigue (orch. Stokowski)

PO	19/4/37	V 1943	DA 1637

CANNING, Thomas
Fantasy on a Hymn Theme by Justin Morgan

HSO		*SDBR 3070*

CANTELOUBE, Joseph
Songs of the Auverne
   Moffo

ASO	pub. 1965	*LSC 2795*

CESTI, Marc Antonio
Tu Mancavi a Tourmentarmi Crudelissima Speranza
(orch. Stokowski)

SO	28/2/52	*LM 1721*
SOA		*UAS 8001*

CHABRIER, Alexis
España Rhapsody

PO	9/5/19	V 6241(a)	DB 384(a)
NATPO	Nov./75	*PCNH 4*	

CHOPIN, Frédéric
Les Sylphides: Ballet Suite

SO	11/5/50	*VIC 1020*	DB 21255

Mazurka #13 in A Minor (orch. Stokowski)

PO	7/11/37	V 1855	DA 1638
HSO		*SDBR 3070*	
LSO	1975	*SPC 21130*	*PFS 4351*

Mazurka #17 in B Flat Minor (orch. Stokowski)

PO	12/12/37	V M841
NATPO	1976	*CBS 73589*

Prelude #4 in E Minor (orch. Stokowski)

PO	6/11/22	V 1111(a)
SO	8/11/50	*LM 1238*

Prelude #24 in D Minor (orch. Stokowski)
```
PO              7/11/37      V 1998       DA 1639
SO              8/11/50      LM 1238
HSO                          SDBR 3070
NATPO           1976         CBS 73589
```
Waltz #7 in C Sharp Minor (orch. Stokowski)
```
HSO                          SDBR 3070
```

CLARKE, Jeremiah
Prince of Denmark's March (orch. Stokowski)
```
HBSO            30/8/46      V 11-9419    DB 6737   CAL 153
Snell
LSO             1975         SPC 21130    PFS 4351
```

COPLAND, Aaron
Billy the Kid: Prairie Night, Celebration Dance
```
PSONY           3,17/11/47   ML 2167
```

CORELLI, Arcangelo
Concerto Grosso Op. 6 #8, Christmas Concerto
Kipnis
```
SO                           BGS 70696
```

COWELL, Henry
Tales of our Countryside
Cowell
```
ASO             5/7/41       C X235
```
Persian Set
```
SO              29/10/52     CRI 114
```

CRESTON, Paul
Symphony Op. 20: Scherzo
```
ASO             8/7/41       C 11713
```

DAWSON, William
Negro Folk Symphony
```
ASO             pub. 1963    DL 710077
```

DEBUSSY, Claude
Children's Corner Suite (orch. Caplet)
```
SO              2/3/49       LM 9023
                : Three Excerpts
SSO                          SDBR 3108
```
Danses Sacrée et Profane
Philips
```
PO              4/4/31       V M116       DB 1642/3
```
Estampes: Soirée dans Granada (orch. Stokowski)
```
NATPO           1976         CBS 73589
```
Images pour Orchestre: Ibéria
```
FNRSO           pub. 1959    S 60102
```
Nocturnes
```
PO              7/11, 12/12/37,
                9/4/39       V M630       DB 3596      3981/2
                             DA 1742
Shaw Chorale
SO              10/11,
                11/10/50     LM 1154
BBCWC
LSO             pub. 1960    S 60104
                : Nuages
```

```
PO                2/5/29      M 116       DB 1614
        : Fêtes
PO               11/10/27     V 1309      E 507
PO               12/12/37,
                 9/3/39       V 2034    DA 1742    CAL 140
Prélude à l'Après-midi d'un Faune
PO               28/4/24      V 6481(a)   DB 840(a)
PO               10/3/27      V 6696      DB 840
PO               8/12/40      V 17700
SO               4/10/49      LM 1154     DB 21297
SO               pub. 1958    SIB 6094
LSO (live)       14,15/6/72   SPC 21090/1   OPFS 3/4
La Cathédrale engloutie (orch. Stokowski)
PO               30/4/30      V M116
NPO              25/9/65      SPC 21006   SDD 455
Clair de lune (orch. Stokowski)
PO               5/4/37       V 1812    DA 1634    CAL 123
SO               24/5/47      LM 1154
SO               pub. 1958    SIB 6094
NATPO            1976         CBS 73589
La Mer
LSO              22,23/6/70   SPC 21059   PFS 4220


DELIBES, Léo
Sylvia: Valse Lento and Pizzicato
SO               16/5/50      VIC 1020


DOLAN, Robert Emmett
Lady in the Dark (film): A Message for Liza
HBSO             23/8/46      V 10-1302


DUBENSKY, Arcady
The Raven (after Poe)
de Loache
PO               1936         V 2000/1    L 1006 (STD)


DUKAS, Paul
La Péri: Fanfare
SO               2/9/56       SIB 6094
The Sorcerer's Apprentice
PO               7/11/37      V M717      DB 3533/4
PO (arr. Stokowski)          WDX 101     BVS 101


DUPARC, Henri
Ectase
Gray
LSO              1975         SPC 21130   PFS 4351

DVORAK, Antonin
Symphony #9
PO               15/5/25 to
                 8/10/27      V M1      CRI 2 0334
PO               22/10/34     V M273    DB 2543/7    CAL 104
ASO              1940         C M416
SO               30/11/49     LM 1013
NPO              pub. 1975    CRL 2 0334
        : Largo
PO               21/5/19      V 6236(a)
Slavonic Dance Op. 72 #2
CPO              1975         SPC 21117   PFS 4333
```

134

EICHHEIM, Henry
Japanese Nocturne
    PO   1/5/29   V 7260   D 1936
Bali, Symphonic Variations
    PO   circa 1934 V 14141/2

ELGAR, Edward
Variations on an Original Theme, Op 36
    CPO   7/9/72   *SPC 21136*   *PFS 4338*

ENESCO, Georges
Rumanian Rhapsody #1
    SO   1947   V 12-0069   DB 6828
    SO   17/4/53   *LM 1878*
    RCASO   pub. 1961   *LSC 2471*   *SB 2130*
Rumanian Rhapsody #2
    SO   1/10/53   *LM 1878*

FALLA, Manuel de
El Amor Brujo
  Merriman
    HBSO   15/8/46   *VIC 1043*   DB 21039/41

  Verrett
    PO   25/2/60   *Y 32368*   *CBS 61288*
        : Ritual Fire Dance
    ASO   5/7/41   C 11879
La Vida Breve: Spanish Dance
    PO   8/12/28   V 6997   DB 1949
Nights in the Gardens of Spain (live)
  Kapell
    PSONY   13/11/49   *OPUS 71*

FARBERMAN, Harold
Evolution — Part One
    SO   2/9/56   *SSAL 8385*

FRANCK, César
Grande Pièce Symphonique: Andante (orch. O'Connell)
    PO   19/4/37   V 14947
Panis Angelicus (orch. Stokowski)
    PO   15/1/36   V 8964   DB 3318
Symphony in D Minor
    PO   3,4,11/10/27 V M22   D 1404/8   *LM 22 (STD)*
    PO   30/12/35   V M300   DB 3226/31
    HRPO   24,25/8/70   *SPC 21061*   *PFS 4218*

FRESCOBALDI, Girolamo
The Second Book of Gagliards: #2, Gagliarda
    PO   22/10/34   V 1985   DA 1606
    SO   4/4/52   *LM 1721*
    SOA   1958/59   *UAS 8001*

GABRIELLI, Giovanni
Canzon Quartafoni a 15
  Brass Choir, A Cappella Chorus
    SO   6/3/52   *LM 1721*
In Ecclesiis Benedicte Domino
    SO   6/3/52   *LM 1721*

Sonata Pian e Forte (orch. Stokowski)
SOA   *UAS 8001*

GLAZOUNOV, Alexander
Scènes de Ballet: Dance Orientale
PO   2/5/27   V 1335   E 521
Violin Concerto in A Minor (live)
  Marcovici
LSO   14,15/6/72   *SPC 21090/1*   *OPFS 3/4*

GLIERE, Reinhold
The Red Pony: Sailor's Dance
PO   17/3/34   V 1675   DA 1398   *VCM 7101*
                                    VIC 6060
SO   14/2/53   *LM 1816*
Symphony #3, Ilya Mourometz
PO   27/3/40   V M841   *LCT 1106*
HSO   pub. 1958   *S 60089*

GLUCK, Christoph Willibald von
Armide, Musette, Sicilienne
SO   pub. 1958   *SIB 6094*
Iphigénie en Aulide: Lento
SO   pub. 1958   *SIB 6094*
Orfeo: Dance of the Blessed Spirits
PO   8/11/17   V 6238(a)
  : Reigen
SO   pub. 1958   *SP 8458*
  : O Saviour Hear Me
  Luboff Choir,
NSO   pub. 1962   *LSC 2593*

GOEB, Roger
Symphony #3
SO   29/4/52   *LM 1727*   *CRI 120*

GOULD, Morton
Latin-American Symphonette: Guaracha
ASO   July/41   C 11713
Dance Variations
  Whittemore, Lowe
SFSO   22/11/53   *LM 1858*

GOUNOD, Charles
Faust: Kermesse Waltz
PO   1/5/23   V 944(a)   DA 562(a)

GRAINGER, Percy
**Country Gardens, Mock Morris, Shepherd's Hey, Molly on the
Shore, Early one Morning, Irish Tune, Handel in the Strand**
  Percy Grainger
SO   31/4, 8/11/50   *LM 1238*

GRANADOS, Enrique
Goyescas: Intermezzo
SO   11/12/47   *LM 9029*   DB 6915

GRIEG, Edvard
  Peer Gynt: Anitra's Dance
  PO   8/11/17   V 799(a)

GRIFFES, Charles
  Roma♠ Sketches: The White Peacock
  PSONY   3,17/11/47   *ML 2167*

HANDEL, George Frederic
  Alcina: Tamburano
  SO   pub. 1958   *SP 8458*   *SXLP 30174*
  Messiah: Pastoral Symphony
  PO   15/3/30   V 7316   D 1938   *CAL 120*
  SO   27/3/47   V 11-9837
  : Selections
  Armstrong, Proctor, Bowen, Cameron, LSOC
  LSO   29/9/66   *SPC 21014*   *SPA 284*
  Chandos Anthem #2: Overture in D Minor (orch. Stokowski)
  PO   16/12/35   V 1798   D 1556
  Xerxes: Largo
  Luboff Choir
  NSO   pub. 1962   *LSC 2593*
  Water Music — Suite
  PO   1934   V 8550/1   DB 2470/3
  RCASO   pub. 1962   *VICS 1513*   *SB 6522*
  Royal Fireworks Music
  RCASO   pub. 1962   *LSC 2612*   *SB 6522*

HARRISON, Lou
  Suite for Violin, Piano and Small Orchestra
  SO   29/10/52   *LM 1785*   *CRI 114*

HAYDN, Franz Joseph
  The Creation: The Heavens are Telling
  NLC
  NSO   pub. 1962   LSC 2593
  Symphony #53, Imperial
  SO   25/5/49   *LM 1073*
  String Quartet in F Op 3 #5: Serenade (orch. Stokowski)
  PO   4/5/29   V 7256   D 1864   *CAL 120*
  HBSO   30/8/46   V 11-9419   DB 6737   *CAL 120*
  NATPO   Nov./75   *PCNH 4*

HOLST, Gustav
  The Planets
  RWC
  LAPO   1957   *S 60175*   *SMFP 2134*

HUMPERDINCK, Engelbert
  Hänsel and Gretel: Overture
  SO   22/9/49   V 12-1321   DB 21256   *LM 2042*
  : Evening Prayer
  NLC
  NSO   pub. 1962   *LSC 2593*

IBERT, Jacques
  Escales
  SO   15/2/51   *LM 9029*
  FNRSO   pub. 1959   *S 60102*

137

IPPOLITOV–IVANOV, Mikhail
Caucasian Sketches: In the Village
PO	15/5/25	V 6514		
PSONY	3/11/47	C 12759		

: Procession of the Sardar
PO	29/4/22	V 796(a)		
PO	11/10/27	V 1335	E521	*VCM 7101*
		VIC 6060		
NATPO	Nov./75	*PCNH 4*		

IVES, Charles
Orchestral Set #2
LSO	22,23/6/70	*SPC 21060*	*PFS 4203*

Robert Browning Overture
ASO	1965	*MS 7015*

Symphony #4
Katz, Serebrier, Schola Cantorum
ASO	29,30/4/65	*MS 6775*	*CBS 72403*

**They are There! (A War Song March) (choral version); Majority
(all The Masses); An Election (It Strikes Me That); Lincoln, The
Great Commoner**
Gregg Smith Singers, Ithica College Concert Choir
ASO	18/11/67	M 4 32504

JOSTEN, Werner
Concerto Sacro 1—11
David del Tredici
ASO	pub. 1960	*CRI 200*

Jungle, Symphonic Poem
ASO	March/71	*CRI SD 267*

Canzona Seria
ASO	March/71	*SD 267*

KEY, Francis Scott
Star-Spangled Banner (orch. Stokowski)
(Preceded by Pledge to the Flag by Goddard Lieberson)
ASO	circa 1940	C 17204

KHATCHATURIAN, Aram
Masquerade: Suite
PSONY	3/11/47	*ML 4071*

Symphony #2
SOA	1958/59	*UAS 8002*

Symphony #3
CSO	20,22/2/68	*LSC 3067*	*SB 6804*

LEIMER, Kurt
Piano Concerto #4
Leimer
SOA	*IC 063 29030*

LIADOV, Anatol
Eight Russian Folk Dances
PO	17/3/24	V 1681	DA 1415

Dance of the Amazon
PO	8/12/24	V 1112 (a)

138

LISZT, Franz
  Hungarian Rhapsody #1
    NBSCO   8/2/55   *LM 1878*
  Hungarian Rhapsody #2 (orch. Mueller-Berghaus)
    PO   20/5/20   V 6236 (a)
    PO   18/11/26
                   10/3/27   V 6652   D 1296   *VCM 710*
                           VIC 6060
    PO   16/11/36   V 14422   DB 3086
    ASO   1940   C 11646
    NBCSO   8/2/55   *LM 1878*
    RCASO   pub. 1961   *LSC 2471*   *SB 2130*
  Hungarian Rhapsody #3
    NBCSO   10/2/55   *LM 1878*
  Les Préludes
    SO   9/12/47   *LM 1073*

LOEFFLER, Charles
  A Pagan Poem
    SO   pub. 1960   *S 60080*

LULLY, Jean Baptiste
  Alceste: Prelude
    PO   30/4/30   V 7424   DB 1587
  Le Triomphe de l'amor: Nocturne
    PO   30/4/30   V 7424   DB 1587
    SO   4/4/52   *LM 1721*
  Thésée: March
    PO   30/4/30   V 7424   DB 1587
    SO   4/4/52   *LM 1721*

MAHLER, Gustaf
  Symphony #2
    Price, Fassbaender, LSOC
    LSO   1975   *ARL 2 0852*

MARTIN, Frank
  Petite Symphonie Concertante
    SO   pub. 1959   *SP 8597*

McDONALD, Harl
  Concerto for Two Piano and Orchestra
    Behrend, Kelberine
    PO   19/4/37   V M557   DB 5700/2
  Legend of the Arkansas Traveller
    PO   27/3/40   V 18069   *CAL 235*
  Festival of Workers: Dance of the Workers
    PO   25/11/35   V 8919   DB 2913
  Symphony #2: Rhumba
    PO   25/11/35   V 8919   DB 2913

MENDELSSOHN, Felix
  A Midsummer Night's Dream: Scherzo
    PO   8/11/17   V 7456 (a)
    ASO   11/7/41   C 1198

MENOTTI, Gian-Carlo
  Sebastian: Ballet Suite
    NBCSO   28/9/54   *LM 1858*

MESSIAEN, Oliver
  L'Ascension
    PSONY   17/11/47   *ML 4214*

    LSOC
    LSO   22, 23/6/70 *SPC 21060*   *PFS 4203*

MOZART, Wolfgang Amadeus
  German Dance #3 K509
    SO   17/9/48   *LM 1238*
  Piano Concerto #21 K467 (live)
    Hess
    PSONY   1949   *MJA 1967- 1B*
  Piano Sonata #11 K331: Turkish March (orch. Stokowski)
    NBCSO   9/2/55   *LM 2042*
  Don Giovanni: Overture
    NATPO   March/76   *PCNHX 6*
  Serenade #10 For 13 Wind Instruments K361
    Soloists from the ASO
    ASO   *VSD 71158*
  Sinfonia Concertante in E Flat K297b
    PO   22/12/40   V M 760   DB 10118/21   *CAL 123*
  Symphony #40 K550: Minuetto
    PO   9/5/19   V 74609 (a)   DB 385 (a)

MUSSORGSKY, Modeste
  Boris Godunov: Symphonic Synthesis (orch. Stokowski)
    PO   16/11/36   V M391   DB 3244/6
    ASO   4, 5/7/41   C M516
    SRO   12/9/68   *SPC 21032*   *PFS 4181*
           : Excerpts
    Rossi-Lemini
    SFSO   8, 10/12/52 *LM 1764*
  Khovantschina: Prelude, Act 1/Dance of the Persian Slaves
    SO   26/2/53   *LM 1816*
           : Entracte, Act IV
    PO   12/12/22   V 6366 (a)   DB 599 (a)
    PO   12/10/27   V 6775   D 1427
    SO   14/4/53   *LM 1816*
    NATPO   Nov./75   *PCNH 4*
  Pictures at an Exhibition (orch. Stokowski)
    PO   27/11/39   V M706   DB 5827/30
                1941   C M511
    NPO   25/9/65   *SPC 1006*   *PFS 4095*
         : Hut on Fowls Legs, Great Gate at Kiev (orch. Ravel.)
    SO   3/9/56   *SIB 6094*
  Night on Bald Mountain (orch. Stokowski)
    PO   8/12/40   V 17900   DB 5900   *VCM 7101*
                           VIC 6060
    PO   1940   *WDX 101*   *BVS 101*
    SO   14/2/53   *LM 1816*
    LSO   16/6/67   *SPC 21026* *PFS 4139*

NOVACEK, Ottkar
  Perpetuum Mobile (orch. Stokowski)
    PO   8/12/40   V 18069   *CAL 123*
    ASO   5/7/41   C 11879
    NATPO   1976   CBS 73589

140

OFFENBACH, Jacques
Tales of Hoffman: Barcarolle
HBSO   1945   V 11-9174 DB 10130

ORFF, Carl
Carmina Burana
Babikian, Gardner, Hager, Chorus
HSO   pub. 1959 *S 60236*

PAGANINI, Niccolò
Moto Perpetuo
SO   pub. 1958 *SP 8415* *SXLP 30174*

PALESTRINA, Giovanni
Adoramus te
PO   12/11/34 V 11-8576 DB 6260
SO   4/4/52 *LM 1721*
SOA   1958/59 *UAS 8001*
Bone Jesu
SO   26/3/52 *LM 1721*

PANUFNIK, Andrzej
Universal Prayer
Cantelo, Watts, Mitchinson, Stalman, Louis Halsey Singers,
N. Kynaston
    4, 5/9/70 *RHS 305*

PERSICHETTI, Vincent
Divertimento for Band: March
SO   2/9/56 *SSAL 8385*

PONCHIELLI, Amilcare
La Gioconda: Dance of the Hours (orch. Stokowski)
PO   1940 *WDX 101* *BVS 101*

POULENC, Francis
Concerto Champêtre for Harpsichord and Orchestra (live)
Wanda Landowska
PSONY   6/11/49 *IPL 106/7*

PROKOFIEF, Serge
Cinderella: Ballet Suite
SSO   *SDBR 3106*
Love for Three Oranges: Infernal Scene, March, Prince and the Princess
NBCSO   27/11/41 V 18497 DB 6151
Peter and the Wolf
Rathbone
ASO   1940 *CL 671*
    : plus Orchestral Suite
Keeshan
SSO   *SDBR 3043*
Romeo and Juliet: Suite
NBCSO   5, 7/10/54 *LM 2117*
Ugly Duckling
Resnik
SSO   *SDBR 3108*
Symphony #5
USSRO   pub. 1961 *MK 1551*

141

PURCELL, Henry
Dido and Aeneas: When I am Laid in Earth (orch. Stokowski)
SO   25/7/50   *LM 1875*
King Arthur: Hornpipe
SO   pub. 1958   *SIB 6094*

RACHMANINOFF, Serge
Piano Concerto #2: 2nd & 3rd Mov'ts.
Rachmaninoff
PO   3/1/24   V 8064/5/6 (a)   DB 747/9 (a)
              : complete
Rachmaninoff
PO   10/4/29   V M58   DB 1333/7   *AVM 3 0296*
Prelude in C# Minor Op. 3 #2 (arr. Stokowski)

CPO   1975   *SPC 21130*
Rhapsody on a Theme of Paganini
Rachmaninoff
PO   24/12/34   V M250   DB 2426/8   *AVM 3 0296*
Symphony #3
NATPO   May/75   *DSM 1007*
Vocalise (arr. Dubensky)
SO   25/2/53   *LM 2042*
SO   pub. 1958   *SP 8415*   *SXLP 30174*

Moffo
ASO   pub. 1965   *LSC 2975*   *SB 6804*
NATPO   May/75   *DSM 1007*

RAVEL, Maurice
Alborada del gracioso
FNRSO   pub. 1959   *S 60102*
Bolero
ASO   26/7/40   C X174
Daphnis and Chloë: Suite #2
LSOC
LSO   22, 23/6/70   *SPC 21061*   *PFS 4220*
L'Eventail de Jeanne: Fanfare
HRPO   24, 25/8/70   *SPC 21061*   *PFS 4218*
Rapsodie espagnole
PO   17/3/34   V 8282/3   DB 2367/8
LSO   pub. 1960   *S 60104*

RESPIGHI, Ottorino
The Pines of Rome
SOA   *UAS 8001*

REVUELTAS, Silvestre
Sensemaya
SO   11/12/47   V 12-0470   DB 6915

RIMSKY-KORSAKOV, Nicolas
Ivan the Terrible: Prelude to Act III (arr. Stokowski)
PO   9/4/39   V M717
NATPO   1976   *CBS 73589*
Russian Easter Festival Overture
PO   26/1/29   V 7018/9   D 1676/7   *L 002*   (STD)
                          VCM 7101   *VIC 6060*
NBCSO   23/4/42   V M937   DB 6173/4

142

Moscona
SO	16/4/53	*LM 1816*	
CSO	20, 22/2/68	*LSC 3067*	*SB 6804*

Snow Maiden: Dance of the Tumblers
PO	19/3/23	V 6431 (a)

Capriccio Espagnol
NPO	rel. 1976	*SPC 21117*	*PFS 4333*

Scheherazade
PO	8, 10, 12, 13/10/27	V M23	D 1436/40
PO	8/10/34	V M269	DB 2522/7
PHO	23/5, 14, 15/6/51	*LM 1732*	*ALP 1339*
LSO	22/9/64	*SPC 21005*	*PFS 4062*
RPO	pub. 1976	*ARL I 1182*	

: Festival at Bagdad
PO	9/3/19	V 6246 (a)

: The Young Prince and Princess
PO	25/3/21	V 6246 (a)

Tsar Saltan: Flight of the Bumble Bee
NATPO	1976	*CBS 73589*

ROSSINI, Gioacchino
William Tell: Overture
NATPO	March/76	*PCNHX 6*

SAINT-SAËNS, Camille
Carnival of Animals
Montgomery, Barabini
PO	26, 27/9/29	V M71	D 1992/4

Behrend, Levin, B. Heifetz
PO	27/11/39	V M785	DB 5942/4 *CAL 100*

Danse Macabre
PO	29/4/25	V 6505	D 1121
PO	15/1/36	V 14162	DB 3077 *VCM 7101*
		VIC 6060	
NATPO	Nov./75	*PCNH 4*	

Samson and Delilah: Bacchanale
PO	6/1/20	V 6241 (a)	DB 384 (a)
PO	13/10/27	V 6823	D 1807 *VCM 7101*

: Excerpts
Peerce, Stevens, Merrill, Shaw Chorale
NBCSO	7, 14/9/54	*LM 1848*	*ALP 1308*

SATIE, Erik
Gymnopedies 1 and 3 (orch. Debussy)
PO	12/12/37	V 1965	DA 1688

SCHOENBERG, Arnold
Gurrelieder (live)
Althouse, Bampton, Betts, Robofsky, Vreeland, de Loache,
Princeton Glee Club, Fortnightly Club, Mendelssohn Club
PO	11/4/32	V M127	DB 1769/82	*AVM 2 2017*
	12/4/32		*LM 127 (STD)*	

: Song of the Wood Dove
Lipton
PSONY	28/11/49	*ML 2410*

143

Verklärte Nacht
SO	3/9/52	*LM 1739*	*ALP 1205*
SO	pub. 1960	*S 60080*	

SCHUBERT, Franz
Ave Maria (orch. Stokowski)
PO	1940	*WDX 101*	*BVS 101*

Rosamunde: Ballet in G
PO	11/10/27	V 1312	*CAL 123*

: Overture, Entr'acte Act 3, Ballet in G
SO	10/9/52	*LM 1730*	*ALP 1193*

: Overture
NATPO	March/76	*PCNHX 6*

Moment Musicale #3 (orch. Stokowski)
PO	27/1/22	V 799 (a)		
PO	6/4/27	V 1312	*CAL 123*	
HBSO	1945	V 11-9174	DB 10130	
LSO	1975	*SPC 21130*	*PFS 4351*	

Symphony #8
PO	18/4/24	V 6459/61 (a)	DB 792/4 (a)	
PO	28, 30/4/27	V M16	D 1779/81	*L 11645/6 (STD)*
		PARNASSUS 5		
ASO	10/7/41	C M485		
LPO	9, 10/9/69	*SPC 21042*	*PFS 4197*	

Tyrolean Dances
SO	10/6/49	*LM 1238*

Viennese Dances
PO	1923	V 74814 (a)

SCHUMANN, Robert
Symphony #2
SO	18, 21/7/50	*LM 1194*

Träumerie
ASO	11/7/41	V 11982

SCRIABIN, Alexander
Etude in C Sharp Minor Op. 2 #1 (orch. Stokowski)
SO	*VCS 10095*

Symphony #4, Poem of Ecstasy
PO	19/3/32	V M 125	DB 1706/7	*L 11616/7 (STD)*
HSO		*SDBR 3032*		
CPO	8/9/72	*SPC 21117*	*PFS 4333*	

Symphony #5, Poem of Fire
Curtis Institute Chorus, Levin
PO	19/3/32	V M125	DB 1708/9	*L 11616/7 (STD)*

SHOSTAKOVITCH, Dmitri
Age of Gold: Ballet Suite
CSO	20, 22/2/68	*LSC 3133*	*SB 6839*

Lady Macbeth of Mtsensk: Entr'acte
SOA	1958/59	*UAS 8004*

Prelude #14 in E Flat Major
PO	30/12/35	V M192	DB 2884
ASO	14/11/40	C M446	
SOA	1958/59	*UAS 8004*	
NATPO	1976	*CBS 73589*	

Symphony #1
PO	18/11/33	V M192	DB 2203/7	*LM 192 (STD)*
SOA	1958/59	*UAS 8004*		

Symphony #5
PO	20/4/39	V M619	DB 3991/6	
SSO		*SDBR 3010*		

Symphony #6
PO	8, 28/12/40	V M867		
CSO	20, 22/2/68	*LSC 3133*	*SB 6839*	

Symphony #11
HSO	pub. 1958	*S 60228*	*WRC ST 776/6*

SIBELIUS, Jean

Finlandia
PO	18/4/21	V 6366 (a)	DB 599 (a)	
PO	28/4/30	V 7412	DB 1584	*L 11656 (STD)*
		VCM 7101	*VIC 6060*	
SO	pub. 1958	*SIB 6094*		

The Girl with Roses
PSONY	17/11/47	C 12938

Kuolema: Valse Triste
PO	15/1/36	V 14726	DB 3318	*CAL 123*
SO	11/12/47	*LM 9029*	DB 21555	
SO	4/10/49	*LM 1238*		

Legends, Op. 22: Swan of Tuonela
PO	2, 3/5/29	V 7380	D1997	*L 11656 (STD)*
		VCM 7101	*VIC 6060*	
SO	11/12/47	LM 9029	DB 21555	
SO	pub. 1958	*SIB 6094*		
NATPO	1976	CBS, in preparation		

Symphony #1
SO	11, 13/7/50	*LM 1125*	*ALP 1210*
NATPO	1976	CBS, in preparation	

Symphony #2
NBCSO	15, 16/9/54	*LM 1854*	*ALP 1440*

Symphony #4
PO	23/4/32	V M160	*L 11638/9 (STD)*	*SRS 3001*

The Tempest Op. 109: Berceuse
PO	7/11/37	V 14726	DB 6009
SO	4/10/49	*LM 1038*	DB 21334

SMETANA, Bedrich

The Bartered Bride: Overture
RCASO	pub. 1961	*LSC 2471*	*SB 2130*

Má Vlast: The Moldau
RCASO	pub. 1961	*LSC 2471*	*SB 2130*

SOUSA, John Philip

El Capitan
PO	15/3/30	V 1441	E 556

Stars and Stripes Forever
PO	27/9/29	V 1441	E 556
NATPO	Nov./75	*PCNH 4*	

STILL, William Grant

Afro–American Symphony: Scherzo
ASO	13/11/40	C 11992

STRAUSS, Johann II

Die Fledermaus: Waltzes
HBSO	23/8/46	V 10-1310

The Blue Danube

PO	10/5/19	V 6237 (a)		
PO	10/6/26	V 6584	D 1218	
PO	9/4/39	V 15425	DB 3821	*LM 6074*
SO	22/9/49	V 12-1160		
NBCSO	13/1/55	*LM 2042*		
SO	pub. 1958	*SIB 6094*		

Tales from the Vienna Woods

PO	9/4/39	V 6584	
PO	9/4/39	V 15425	
SO	22/9/49	V 12-1160	DB 1346
NBCSO	9/2/55	*LM 2042*	
NATPO	Nov./75	*PCNH 4*	

STRAUSS, Richard

Don Juan

SSO		*SDBR 3023*

Salome: Dance of the Seven Veils

PO	5/12/21	V 6240 (a)	DB 383 (a)
PO	1/5/29	V 7259/60	D 1935/6 *CAL 254*
SSO		*SDBR 3023*	

Suite in B Flat for Winds Op. 4: Gavotte

SO	3/9/56	*SSAL 8385*

Till Eulenspiegel

SO		*SDBR 3023*

Tod und Verklärung

PO	7/4/34	V M217	DB 2325/6
ASO	3, 4/7/41	C M492	
NYCSO	10/12/44	V M1006	DB 6320/2

STRAVINSKY, Igor

Firebird: Suite

PO	13/10/24, 8/12/24	V 6492/3 (a)	DB 841/2 (a)
PO	12/10/27	V M53	
PO	25/11, 30/12/35	V M291	DB 2882/4
ASO	14/11/40	C M446	
NBCSO	27/4/42	V M933	
SO	24/5/50, 7/6/50	*LM 9029*	
BPO	pub. 1959	*S 60229*	
LSO	16/6/67	*SPC 21026*	*PFS 4139*

Fireworks

PO	6/11/22	V 112 (a)

L'Histoire du Soldat

Singher, Milhaud, Aumont
Stokowski Instrumental
Ensemble pub. 1967   Fr. *VSD 71165*   Eng. *VSD 71166*

Pastorale (orch. Stokowski)

PO	26/11/34	V 1998	
RPO	17/6/69	*SPC 21041*	*PFS 4189*

Petrouchka Suite

PO	19/4/37	V M574	DB 3511 *CAL 203*
SO	30/6, 5/7/50	*LM 1175*	*ALP 1240*
BPO	pub. 1959	*S 60229*	

Le Sacre du Printemps

PO	24/9/29,

| | 12/3/30 | V M74 | D 1919/22 | |
| PO (arr. Stokowski)1940 | | *WDX 101* | *BVS 101* | |

TCHAIKOVSKY, Peter Ilich
Capriccio Italien
| PO | 28, 30/1/29 | V 6949/50 | D 1739/40 | *L 7002 (STD)* |
| LPO | 1975 | *6500 766* | | |

Francesca da Rimini
PSONY	3/11/47	*ML 4071*	*33c 1030*
SSO		*SDBR 3011*	
LSO	1975	*6500 921*	

Hamlet
| SSO | | *SDBR 3011* |

Marche Slav
PO	15/5/25	V 6513	D 1046
HBSO	1/8/45	V 11-9388	*CAL 153*
LSO	16/6/67	*SPC 21026*	*PFS 4139*
LSO (live)	14, 15/6/72	*SPC 21090/1*	*OPFS 3/4*

The Nutcracker: Suite #1
PO	3, 10, 18/11/26	V M3	D 1214/6	*L 7004 (STD)*
PO	26/11/34	V 265	DB 2540/2	*CAL 100*
SO	29/6/50	*LM 9023*	*ALP 1193*	
LPO	1975	*6500 766*		
	: Excerpts		
PO	1940	*WDX 101*	*BVS 101*
	: Dance of the Sugar Plum Fairy		
SO	17/9/48	V 10-1487	
	: Dance of the Flutes		
PO	13/2/22	V 798 (a)	
	: Waltz of the Flowers		
SO	9/5/50	*LM 1083*	DB 21547

1812 Overture
| PO | 29/4/30 | V 7499/500 | DB 1663/4 |

Band of the Grenadier Guards
| RPO | 16, 17/6/69 | *SPC 21041* | *PFS 4189* |

Romeo and Juliet
PO	26, 27/9/28	V M46	DB 1947/9
PSONY	28/11/49	*ML 4273*	*33c 1030*
SRO	12/9/68	*SPC 21032*	*PFS 4181*

String Quartet #1: Andante Cantabile
| SO | pub. 1958 | *SP 8458* | *SXLP 30174* |

Sleeping Beauty: Suite
| SO | 11/11/47 | *V LM1010* | *ALP 1002* |
| NPO | 25/9/65 | *SPC 21008* | *PFS 4085* |

Aurora's Wedding (arr. Diaghilef)
| SO | 8, 9, 14/4/53 | *LM 1774* |

Swan Lake: Dance of the Little Swans, Swan Queen
SO	11/5/50	*LM 1083*
	: Acts II and III		
NBSCO	Oct., Nov. 1954, Jan. 1955	*LM 1894*	*ALP 1443*
	: Suite		
NPO	25/9/65	*SPC 21008*	*PFS 4085*

147

Humoresque Op. 10 #2 (orch. Stokowski)

ASO	10/7/41	C 19005	
NBCSO	23/4/42	V M933	
HBSO	25/7/45	V 11-9187	CAL 153
SO	25/2/53	LM 1774	
NATPO	1976	CBS 73589	

Solitude Op. 73 #6 (orch. Stokowski)

PO	19/4/37	V 14947	
ASO	11/7/41	C 11982	
HBSO	25/7/45	V 11-9187	CAL 153
SO	25/2/53	LM 1774	
NATPO	Nov./75	PCNH 4	

Eugene Onegin: Polonaise

SO	1/10/53	LM 2042	

: Polonaise and Waltz

LPO	1975	6500 766	

: Letter Scene

Albanese

SO	6, 8/2/51	LM 142	BLP 1075

Pater Noster

Luboff Choir

NSO	pub. 1962	LSC 2593	

Song Without Words Op. 40 #6 (orch. Stokowski)

PO	28/4/24	V 1111(a)	
PO	8/12/28	V M71	D 1994
CPO	1975	SPC 21130	PFS 4351

Symphony #4

PO	28/9, 29/9, 8/12/28	V M48	DB 1793/7
NBCSO	27/11/41	V M880	
ASO	26/4/71	VSC 10095	

: Scherzo

SO	2/9/56	SIB 6094	

Symphony #5

PO	12/11/34	V M253	DB 2548/53
SO	10, 13/2/53	LM 1780	
NPO	13/9/66	SPC 21017	SDD 493

: 2nd Mov't.

PO	30/4/23	V 6430/1(a)	
SO	28/3/47	V 11-9574	

Symphony #6

ASO	16/11/40	C M432	
HBSO	25/7/45	V M1105	CAL 152
LSO	pub. 1975	ARL 1 0426	

: 3rd Mov't.

PO	18/4/21	V 6242(a)	

Serenade for Strings: Waltz

PSONY	28/11/49	C MM898	

: Complete

LSO	1975	6500 921	

THOMAS, Ambroise
Mignon: Gavotte

PO	1/5/23	V 944 (a)	DA 562 (a)
PO	4/5/29	V M116	DB 1643

THOMSON, Virgil
The Plow that Broke the Plains

148

HBSO	30/8/46	V M1116
SOA		*VSD 2095*
The River		
SOA		*VSD 2095*

TURINA, Joaquin
la Oracion del Torero
SO	pub. 1958	*SIB 6094*	*SXLP 30174*

VAUGHAN WILLIAMS, RALPH
Fantasia on Greensleeves
PSONY	21/2/49	C MM838

Fantasia on a Theme of Thomas Tallis
SO	3/9/52	*LM 1739*

Symphony #6 in E Minor (original version)
PSONY	21/2/49	*ML 4214*	*CBS 61432*

Symphony #8: Scherzo
SO	2/9/56	*SSAL 8385*

VILLA-LOBOS, Heitor
Bachianas Brasileiras #1: Modinha
SSO		*SDBR 3016*

Bachianas Brasileiras #5
Albanese
SO	6, 8/2/51	*LM 142*

Moffo
ASO	pub. 1965	*LSC 2795*	*LSB 4114*

Uirapuru
SSO		*SDBR 3016*

VIVALDI, Antonio
Concerto Grosso #11 in D Major (arr. Stokowski)
PO	12/11/34	V 14113/4	DB 6047/8
SO	28, 29/2/52	*LM 1721*	

Kipnis
SO		*BGS 10686*

Concerto Op. #8: 1-4, The Four Seasons
Bean
NPO	24/8/66	*SPC 21015*	*PFS 4124*

WAGNER, Richard
Lohengrin: Prelude to Act 1
PO	28/4/24	V 6490 (a)	DB 839 (a)	
PO	13/10/27	V 6791	D 1463	*CAL 120*

  : Prelude to Act III
PO	27/3/40	V M781	DB 5853

Die Meistersinger: Prelude to Act 1
PO	15/1/36	V M731	DB 5852/3
LSO (live)	14,15/6/72	*SPC 21090/1*	*OPFS 3/4*

  : Prelude to Act III
PO	17/3/31	V 1584	DA 1291

Parsifal: Prelude to Act I
PO	28/11/36	V M421	DB 3269/72

  : Act III Symphonic Synthesis
PO	7/4/34	V 8617/8	DB 2272/3

```
SO      24/9/52    LM 1730
HSO                SDBR 3031
        : Act III Good Friday Spell
PO      28/11/36   V M421          DB 3269/72
SO      17/9/52    LM 1730
Rienzi: Overture
PO      8/5/19     V 6239 (a)      DB 382 (a)
PO      18/11/26,
        6/1/27     V 6624/5        D 1226/7
PSONY   17/11/47   ML 2153         33c 1026
Das Rheingold: Symphonic Synthesis
PO      4/4/33     V M179   DB 1976/8    L 11643/4 (STD)
        : Entry of the Gods into Valhalla
PO      1940       M 1063

Arroyo, Ordassy, Parker
SOA     24/4/61    VICS 1301       SB 2148
LSO     26/8/66    SPC 21016       PFS 4116
Die Walküre: Wotan's Farewell and Magic Fire Music
PO      5/12/21    V 6245(a)       DB 387(a)
        : Magic Fire Music
PO      9/4/39     V 15800         DB 3942      VCM 7101
                   VIC 6060
PSONY   17/11/47   ML 2153         33c 1026
HSO                SDBR 3070
        : Symphonic Synthesis incl. Wotan's Farewell
Tibbett
PO      30/4/34    V M248          DB 2470/3
        : Ride of the Valkyries
PO      25/3/21    V 6245(a)       DB 387(a)

Arroyo, Ordassy, Yarick, Allen, Okerson, Sarfaty,
Verrett, Parker
SOA     24/4/61    VICS 1301       SB 2148
LSO     26/8/66    SPC 21016       PFS 4116
Siegfried: Symphonic Synthesis
Davis, Jagel
PO      1936       V M441
        : Forest Murmurs
HBSO    1946       V 11-9418       DB 21238     CAL 153
LSO     26/8/66    SPC 21016       PFS 4116
Die Götterdämmerung: Rhine Journey, Funeral Music,
Immolation, Closing Scene
Davis
PO      25/3, 29/4/33 V M188       LM 188 (STD)
LSO     (orch. only)
        pub. 1976  ARL 1 1317
                   : Siegfried's Rhine Journey, Funeral
                     March
PSONY   4/4/49     ML 4273
LSO     26/8/66    SPC 21016       PFS 4116
        : Closing Scene
PO      6/1/27     V 6625          D 1227       VCM 7101
                   VIC 6060

Tannhäuser: Overture, Venusberg Music
PO      23/9/29, 14/3,
        29/4/30    V M78     D 1905/7    LM 11669/70 (STD)
```

Chorus
| PO | 12/12/37 | V M530 | DB 3775/7 |
| SO | 1/2/50 | *LM 1066* | |

Chorus
| SOA | 24/4/61 | *VICS 1301* | *SB 2148* |

: Overture (Dresden Version)
| PO | 7/11/21, | | |
| | 5/12/21 | V 6244/ 6478 (a) | DB 386/7 (a) |

: Grand March
| PO | 28/4/24 | V 6478(a) | |

: Prelude to Act III
| PO | 15/1/36 | V M530 | DB 3254/5 |
| SO | 1/2/50 | V DM1383 | |

: Pilgrims' Chorus
Luboff Choir
| NSO | pub. 1962 | *LSC 2593* | |

Tristan and Isolde: Symphonic Synthesis
PO	16/4/32	V M154	DB 1911/4	*L 11636/7 (STD)*
PO	16,30/12/36,			
	5/4/37	V M508	DB 3087/9	
SO	17/10,			
	9/11/50	*LM 1174*		

: Love Music
ASO	4/11/40,		
	13/12/40	C M427	
PSONY	25/2/60	*MS 6147*	*SCFL 107*

: Act III, Prelude
| SOA | 24/4/61 | *VICS 1301* | *SB 2148* |

Wesendonck Lieder
Farrell
| SO | 22/5/50 | *LM 1066* | |

: Numbers 3, 4, 5
Traubel
| PO | 22/12/40 | V M872 | |

WEBER, Ben
Symphony on Poems of William Blake
Galjour
| SO | 30,31/10/52 | *LM 1785* | *CRI 120* |

WEBER, Carl Maria von
Invitation to the Dance (orch. Weingartner)
| PO | 9/5/19 | V 6237(a) | |

: (orch. Berlioz/Stokowski)
PO	2/5/27	V 6643	DA 1285	
PO	19/4/37	V 15189	DB 3699	*CAL 123*
ASO	13,17/12/40	C 11481		
SO	9/5/50	*LM 1083*		

Stokowski Speaks: Stokowski's "Outline of Themes" and spoken introductions were included in the following sets:

BEETHOVEN
| **Symphony #6** | | *LM 1830* | |
| **Symphony #7** | 30/4/27 | V M17 | |

BRAHMS
Symphony #1   30/4/27   V M15

DVORAK
Symphony #9   6/10/27   V M1   *CRL 2-0334*

FRANCK
Symphony in D Minor 6/10/27   V M22

SCHOENBERG
Gurrelieder   4/5/32   V M127

ANONYMOUS
Two Ancient Liturgical Melodies (sixteenth century)
    PO   1934   V 1789   DA 1551
Deep River
    Luboff Choir
    NSO   pub. 1962   *LSC 2593*
Doxology (The Old 104th)
    Luboff Choir
    NSO   pub. 1962   *LCS 2593*
Russian Christmas Music
    PO   22/10/34   V 1692
    SO   27/3/47   V 11-9837
Etenraku: Eighteenth Century Japanese Ceremonial Prelude
    (orch. Kunoye)
    PO   circa 1934   V 14142

Index

(of persons mentioned in the text)

153